On toddlers: "Two-year-olds are re̶ OshKosh overalls and brand-new ̶ ̶ ̶ ̶ ̶ ̶ and short chunky little legs and sweet little raspy voices that call you Daddy. They're so cute when they stand in front of you, hands on nonexistent hips, bellowing out an adamant NO!, we actually laugh."

On high school dating: "Frankly, it doesn't matter to me if his hair goes down to his butt or is clipped marine-close to the scalp. It doesn't matter if he's got a nose ring or a class ring, a BMW or a bicycle, a leather jacket or a tweed sport coat. He's come to steal her heart. So he's dangerous."

On teenage boys: "I love the way they knock over the furniture of our lives as they move toward adulthood. . . . I have no illusions about their innocence."

On family dinners: "It is right there, between the bread and the butter, where all the great events in life occur, where we make stupid faces at each other and change the course of history, where we catch the sparkling eye of someone who loves us not for what we do or even what we are, but only because we're there, like we're there every day, because we belong there and nowhere else."

(more . . .)

STEVEN LEWIS writes on fathering issues for leading newspapers and magazines from coast to coast. Between doing that and raising an ever-growing family, he teaches writing and literature at Empire State College in New Paltz, New York. In all of the above, Lewis finds pleasures of the most profound kind.

Zen
AND THE ART OF
Fatherhood
LESSONS FROM A
MASTER DAD

Steven Lewis

Ⓟ

A PLUME BOOK

PLUME
Published by the Penguin Group
Penguin Books USA Inc., 375 Hudson Street,
New York, New York 10014, U.S.A.
Penguin Books Ltd, 27 Wrights Lane,
London W8 5TZ, England
Penguin Books Australia Ltd, Ringwood,
Victoria, Australia
Penguin Books Canada Ltd, 10 Alcorn Avenue,
Toronto, Ontario, Canada M4V 3B2
Penguin Books (N.Z.) Ltd, 182–190 Wairau Road,
Auckland 10, New Zealand

Penguin Books Ltd, Registered Offices:
Harmondsworth, Middlesex, England

Published by Plume, an imprint of Dutton Signet,
a division of Penguin Books USA Inc.
Previously published in a Dutton edition.

First Plume Printing, June, 1997
10 9 8 7 6 5 4 3 2 1

"Moon Birth" originally appeared in the *Poughkeepsie Journal*. "Nothing Is to Blame" originally
appeared in *Exits off a Tollroad*, Pentagram, 1974. "Have a Cigar!" originally appeared in *L.A.
Parent*. "Circumcisio" originally appeared in *Seattle's Child*. "Bayou Grace" originally appeared
in *Parents Magazine*. "The Zen of Diaper Dunking" and "The Rules of the Road" originally
appeared in the *Huguenot Herald*. "Who Wears the Belt in Your Family?" "Seven Facts for
Father's Day," and "Zen and the Teenage Girl" originally appeared in *Dutchess Magazine*.
"Where's Papa?" originally appeared in *New York Newsday*. "Outside the Garden" originally
appeared in *The Reporter*. "The Zen of Getting Clean in Rural Connecticut" originally appeared
in the *New York Daily News*. "A Father's Numerology" originally appeared in *Wisconsin*.
"Biting Off the Matter with a Smile" originally appeared in *Commonweal*. "When Bad Things
Happen to Innocent Children" originally appeared in *Parenting Magazine*. "Looking Out for
Number One, Two, Three . . ." originally appeared in the *New York Times Magazine*.

The Library of Congress has catalogued the Dutton edition as follows:

Lewis, Steven M.
    Zen and the art of fatherhood : lessons from a master dad / Steven Lewis.
       p.   cm.
    ISBN 0-525-94147-9 (hc.)   ISBN 0-452-27651-9 (pbk.)
    1. Fathers—United States—Anecdotes.   2. Fatherhood—Religious aspects—Zen Buddhism.
    I. Title
HQ756.L493   1996
306.874'2—dc20   96-3783
                                                                                 CIP

Printed in the United States of America
Original hardcover design by Leonard Telesca

CONTENTS

FOREWORD

Fathering is a dreamy road trip full of contradiction and paradox, meandering summer lanes behind the leather-wrapped wheel of a green Alfa Romeo that become—in a wet sneeze—windy mountain passes slick with ice as you steer a beige Astrovan full of screaming kids. Every time you think that you know where you are, you're not there anymore.

For me, becoming a father—and being a daddy—has sometimes felt like getting lost in Queens. You know you're in New York City, but frankly it doesn't look like it's supposed to look—and at least half the people on the street don't speak the same language or dialect as you—and admitting that you're disoriented to the scowling presence on your right is more than your pride can bear—and, anyway, you're not really lost, you simply need to find a familiar landmark. So you just keep driving. As Tobias Wolff's clueless stepfather says in *This Boy's Life*, "I know a thing or two about a thing or two. . . ."

A thing or two.

As such, fatherhood to me is the perfect oxymoron, pure contradiction. *Zen.* And like Zen, there's no adequate way to describe it. Alan Watts says, "Zen Buddhism is a way and a view of life which does not belong to any of the formal categories of modern Western thought. It is not religion or philosophy; it is not psychology or a type of science. . . ." Neither is the art of fathering.

I am a man who, through something akin to serendipity, has found himself at the wheel of the family Vanagon sputtering across some vast unknown highway where it seems I am doomed to seek what I never shall find; where ambition and purpose is exposed daily as vanity and vexation; but where dark purposelessness is revealed to me through my restless family as crystalline joy.

Over the past twenty-six years, as family matters have grown exponentially more complicated and busier with the birth of each of our seven children, my inner life has paradoxically become simpler and quieter. Is that Zen? I don't know. In 1977 when my third daughter was born and the children suddenly outnumbered my wife and me by a ratio of two to one, I awoke to the knowledge that, despite any illusions to the contrary, we were no longer in control of the family. That's when all my notions about what it means to be a father dropped like a toy boat over a raging waterfall—leaving me sharing a crowded inner tube floating down a slow-moving creek with an extraordinary feeling of freedom. And it was then that I began to grasp the elusive notion, as expressed by Alan Watts, that the "perfection of Zen—or *fatherhood*—is to be perfectly and simply human." Nothing more. And as Hermann Hesse wrote in *Siddhartha*, "everything is necessary." Everything.

I'm sometimes told that as a father of seven I appear to have the wisdom of the ages. To my kids, however, I am as big a fool as I am a wise man. And to my inner self (and often to my wife Patti), I am a pure fool foolishly tripping over myself trying to play the role of the wise man.

Yet in the end—as in the end of another day in which I ponder the imponderables of a life with seven children—I feel like I
really do have some enlightened experience to share with other
fathers who find themselves as lost in this whole inscrutable
process as I am.

1

Before Father Time

MY FATHER, MYSELF

How I learned the value of presence from a father who was rarely around

> *No snowflake falls in an inappropriate place.*
> —ZEN SAYING

My father was not what you might call a New Age nineties dad. When I rewind the boyhood tape, the only moving image I can conjure up is the distinctly 1950s look and smell of my businessman father going to work each morning: the row of brown and gray suits in the closet, the white starched collar, the smell of Aqua Velva, the dark tie pulled off a crowded rack, the big Windsor knot, the heavy herringbone overcoat, the line of hats on the top shelf in the hall closet. And then the door closing. After a long day in which my young life went through more changes than a chameleon—and still stayed the same—the rough scrape of his face when he came in from the cold late each night lingered for hours.

He was a dad. A man. He worked. He worked in New York City from early morning to midevening six days a week. And when he came home, he ate dinner alone and then sat down in the den in front of the black-and-white Sylvania television and did paperwork. Sundays he tended to the lawn or fixed the radiators or regrouted the tiles in the bathroom—and then did more paperwork. The closest we came to doing "stuff" together was when he'd call me all the way into the house from a tight stickball or football game on the street to run down to the basement and get him a wrench or a hammer.

That was it.

Or at least pretty much what I recall about me and my dad when I was growing up in suburban Roslyn Heights, New York. Except that he used to hold my hand while we drove silently in the car.

Not that I expected anything else. He was just like my uncles (Mac, Murray, and Herman), who were scattered around Long Island. And he was no different from Mr. Jayson down on Westwood Circle or Mr. Weil and Mr. Diamond across Candy Lane (yes, Candy Lane), good men who never once strolled into the games that boys play to learn how to be men. They were men. They worked all the time.

The men in my neighborhood didn't go on fishing trips with their sons. They didn't play punchball in their shirtsleeves out on the quiet streets. They didn't lie out on the grass on buggy summer nights, fireflies lighting up the air, watching for meteors and talking earnestly about the possibility of life on other planets. They didn't sit on the edges of our beds on cold winter nights reading chapters of *The Call of the Wild* or *The Hardy Boys*. They didn't go to our Little League games. And years later, long after the first solitary shave and the last innocent kiss, they didn't take us out to the local tavern for a coming-of-age drink and some gravelly man talk about girls and women and children and work. They worked.

And somewhere along the unbroken line—after I left for college in Wisconsin and realized that the textures of life differed according to geography and circumstance—I felt the reconstructed loneliness of a lost boyhood without a fabled Norman Rockwell dad. I promised myself that when I married and had kids I wouldn't allow my days and nights to be consumed in work—no matter what the cost. I would not get trapped in Kenneth Patchen's "murder into pennies round" of daily existence. I'd be free, I'd be around, a kiss on the top of their heads, a hand on their shoulders, an encouraging slap on the butt. I'd go to Little League games, I'd take them to concerts, I'd play ball, I'd go fishing, I'd lean back in bed and read a chapter to them each night, I'd laugh with them until my sides ached: I'd be a pal for my children.

And then I got married and had kids and more kids (and even more kids), and I changed diapers and danced with toddlers on my feet and played ball and went fishing and agonized with them through recitals and blowout soccer games and laughed until my sides ached, and even sat around scraping out the insides of Oreos and ruminating about life and love. But along the way I also discovered that I'd never be their pal.

I learned that unsettling truth as my oldest son, Cael, and Randy McCrory made a secret clubhouse in the barn (and didn't invite me in); as my oldest daughter Nancy and her friend Eva whispered and giggled behind closed doors from night till morning (and didn't let me in on the joke); as Addie fell head over heels in love with another *man* (Tony Ciliberto) in seventh grade; as one by one (by one) my children grew up and found their own pals beyond the solid walls of this house with whom they rightly shared their suddenly private lives.

And through their silence I found out that being a pal isn't the essence—or the alpha and the omega—of fatherhood. Friendship is nice, like icing or gravy, but it's not *it*. *It*, it turns out, is mostly about going to work and coming home each night. It's about being around. Like a dad. Like my dad.

Somewhere along the meandering parental way I understood that what my children want most from me—aside from money and rides and carte blanche to do anything they want—is to be there as they walk through the kitchen door panting and sweaty and hungry for dinner, or when they call home for a ride late Friday night, or as a cushion to lean into on the couch while the

TV does its mindless work. Or, like my father, to reach over out of nowhere and hold their hand in the car when there is nothing in the world to say to each other.

More than forty years later I can still feel his big rough hand holding my small smooth paw as we drove silently in the Chevy station wagon. The truth is that I had nothing to say to him. And, as far as I can figure, he had nothing to say to me. I don't think we knew each other very well when I was a kid. He just held my hand. He treasured me. He let me know that no snowflake falls in an inappropriate place, that I was his.

My father, who it seems was never there, taught me the Zen value of presence: how to not be there and be there at the same time.

SOMETHING IN THE
WAY SHE MOVES

Stumbling into love

*Wind moving through grass so that grass quivers. This
moves me with an emotion that I don't even understand.*
—KATHERINE MANSFIELD

Patti's a patrician, a blue blood, raised in the Garden District of
New Orleans, groomed at Miss Edith Akins Little School and
later refined at the Louise S. McGhee School on Prytannia Street.
She actually understands noblesse oblige.

I'm a New York Jew, spawned out of the generational pickle
juice of Brooklyn and raised in a suburban development of
quarter-acre ranches bulldozed out of a Long Island potato
field. I went to public school in a cranky yellow bus, scratched
my way through Wheatley High in an ugly succession of mohair
sweaters, and learned about obligations by way of the adolescent charms of a girl named Judy Goldstein.

Patricia Charlee Henderson and I met purely by accident
in September 1964 as newly arrived freshmen at the University
of Wisconsin. I thought she was beautiful: gorgeous face, long
brown hair, the sway of her back that left me with a permanent
yearning in the hollow of my throat. I have no idea what she
thought about me, but it wasn't until more than three years

later—a long uninteresting story—that we had our first date: December 10, 1967.

I know the exact date because I had two tickets to see the great Otis Redding. That night Mr. Redding's plane crashed into the frozen waters of Lake Mendota. Certainly an inauspicious beginning to the relationship, but we nevertheless were married the following August.

Twenty-six years later I still don't understand. We have none of the ordinary things in common. Nothing. Sports, plays, music . . . nothing. (I later found out that she didn't even like Otis Redding.) I speak only for myself then when I say I am drawn to her daily in vast unspeakable ways, a vague sense of biological inevitability when we pass in separate cars. Or later when I inhale her scent. Her breath in my ear.

I like her. I like who she is. We somehow share the same vision of life. Beyond that it's pure mystery.

If you'd have asked me to describe my ideal partner twenty-six years ago, it could have been almost anyone but Patti Henderson. ("Beautiful but not my style.") Yet since the moment I first haltingly placed my lips on hers, she was the one with whom I always had to be. No one else. No one else. I can't repeat that too many times.

I have tried in vain to explain to my friends and even some nosy strangers about the desire and the ambivalence at the root of a relationship that not only permanently connected us but inspired us enough to bring seven children into this world. As Stella says to Blanche in *A Streetcar Named Desire*, "There are things that happen between a man and a woman in the dark. . . ."

Things.

And, mostly, things in the dark, though I don't only mean things sexual. There's much more than that. Much more. Although it's hard to be more specific. Patti and I are together all this time *and* have seven kids because of who we are and who we are to each other. As far as I can see there is no more acceptable explanation for our choices than there is about why some people like their oysters from the Chesapeake and others from the Rockies.

And to give this fishy stew a really bizarre flavor, let me add this: while Patti always wanted a large family—it was from the earliest awareness of her sense of connection to the earth—I know myself well enough to realize that had I married someone else, I probably wouldn't have had so many children. It's even possible that I would actually have married someone who didn't want kids and would be now writing a reflection on our matched pair of Harley Sportsters.

But of course I didn't.

Cael was born while we were still undergraduates in Madison. Two years after Nancy graced our lives in Milwaukee, we had Addie in upstate New York. Then Clover. Then Danny. Then Bay. Six years ago Elizabeth Bayou-Grace completed the set. (I think.) Every day I wake up amazed at it all.

It looks like it should make sense.

But after all these years, I still don't get it.

FAMOUS ZEN LAST WORDS I

*"I will not marry until
I'm at least thirty-five."*

Words, as is well known, are great foes of reality.
—JOSEPH CONRAD

It is early November 1967. My college roommate and I are sitting in Ella's Delicatessen on State Street in Madison, Wisconsin. I can't remember now whether it is very early morning or very late evening—probably both—but it's cold and dark outside and I'm on my fifth or sixth cup of java, running at the mouth and soberly contemplating the meaning of life as only fourth-year sophomores can do without feeling completely ashamed of themselves.

I am twenty, in unrequited lust with a provocatively strange and morose brunette named Jodi who has just given me the heave-ho for not being quite strange or morose enough. To complete the picture, I am bent over in my finest sensitive poet's pose, sucking on a Lucky Strike between gulps of coffee and liberally quoting from Hermann Hesse's hippie classic *Siddhartha*, a book I carried in my hip pocket like a flask from 1965 to 1968.

There may have been no more earnest person in Ella's at that moment. There may also have been no less earnest person in

Ella's at all. If I remember correctly, the late sixties turned unc-
tuousness into a public art form.

Anyway, we were slurping up the coffee and blowing out the
smoke and no doubt talking about the cruel and meaningless
cycle of life, the vainglorious, futile despair of bourgeois American materialism, and, of course, freedom—our three favorite sub-
jects—when my roommate asked what I thought of marriage.

Which is when I uttered my undeniable vow, spoken with all
the conviction of an antiwar placard: "Marriage is a middle-class
trap. I guarantee you that I won't get married until I'm at least
thirty-five."

I said that without even a facial tic, without a moment's reflection that it might not be true. I was that sure. After all, I was
twenty, my tuition and rent were paid by my utterly confused
mother and father who lived a thousand miles away, and I was
as free as a cold Wisconsin breeze across the vast prairie—and
determined to stay that way until I was too old to make it matter
anymore. Which was thirty-five.

Until that fateful point, freedom was the only state of existence worth pursuing. My first obligation was to live. Really live.
Be alive. Be on the road. Be me.

It was commonly assumed back then that life was, for all in-
tents and purposes, over on your thirtieth birthday. You sold
out or were sold out. Either way, you were no longer trustworthy.
And by thirty-five you were so far gone—so unfree, so uncool—
that it didn't matter anymore whether you got married or not.
I'd seen countless others trade in their black T-shirts and black
Levi's and engineer boots for white V-necked undershirts and
Hush Puppies and Sansabelt slacks. I'd watched as the hippest
of the hip, the most angst-ridden of a generation of sufferers,
climbed that fateful hill and walked down the other side in poly-
ester suits with plastic smiles on their close-shaved faces, striding
hopefully toward nine-to-five corporate jobs, wives in curlers,
2.3 children, Chevy wagons, Levitt houses, riding mowers, golf
in jackass pants, and, all in all, the paunchy side of life.

At thirty-five, I would stop smoking. I would stop drinking. I would go to sleep after the eleven o'clock news. I would settle down, marry, and die.

My roommate nodded forlornly.

And, as long as I was on a roll, I took a long drag on the Lucky, rolled the smoke up through my nostrils, and blew it out through my dark bearded lips in a thin blue line, muttering like one of Hemingway's Lost Generation heroes, "And I will never have kids. Never." Affecting the high moral tone, which may have been the most useful thing I learned as an undergraduate, I said, "It would be a terrible thing, the cruelest of jokes, to bring an innocent baby into such a painful existence. A world fraught with war, disease, phoniness. Ultimate meaninglessness. [Yes, I believe I used the word *fraught*.] Never."

He understood totally. Of course. He was as miserable as I was. And that was that. I pushed the burning butt into the overflowing tin ashtray and dropped a few crumpled dollars on the table, and we walked back through the silent streets to our apartment and slept till noon.

Three weeks later I tripped and fell hopelessly in love with my roommate's ex-girlfriend, the girl he never wanted to see again. Patti. The attraction was as transforming as it was unintended, but that was the end of our deep understanding—and the end of our friendship. Freedom be damned. I was in love! And nine months later I found myself standing in a living room in New Orleans with a haircut, a trimmed beard, a white linen suit, watching the most beautiful girl I had ever seen in my life walking my way in a white wedding gown.

And ten months after that, July 17, 1969, three days before a man walked on the moon, Cael Devin Lewis was born at St. Mary's Hospital in Madison, thus proving that words are indeed great foes of reality. And thus the quasi-Zen koan: Never say never without saying never.

I've told that story to all my children and to countless thousands of students over the years. All in the name of teaching them the truth. They actually think it's funny or cute or whatever—or they pretend it's funny or cute—and then toss the intended aphorism into the garbage with An apple a day . . . and A stitch in time . . . and the rest of the bourgeois nonsense adults heave their way. They'll learn.

MMM, HE SMELLS GOOD, THIS ONE

The earthy wisdom of southern grandmothers and the power of good gumbo

> *Everything in the universe is connected, everything is osmosis.*
>
> —TAISEN DESHIMARU

I knew immediately upon stepping out of the plane into the thick hot air that I was a fish out of water—or, more appropriately, since fish could probably live in the humid atmosphere of the delta, I was simply out of my element, a wooly panting mutt whose paws get stuck in the swampy muck every time he tries to take a step.

I was dizzy. I was sweaty. I was close to an out-of-body experience.

I was in Louisiana to meet Patti's mother and father—and grandmothers and aunts and uncles and cousins and friends and ex-boyfriends—a daunting task for an aggressively shy beatnik poet whose social graces might best be called stunted.

And soon enough I was failing miserably at the task of winning over my new family. Though Patti's mother, Nancy, loved me immediately for reasons that remain way beyond my comprehension, my tongue grew swollen when I tried to talk with Cousin Bobby or Uncle Bruce and his wife, Red. My ears filled with swamp water when I tried to understand the lilting voices of Patti's friends Clydia, Kingsley, and Amalie. I squirmed and sweated like a malaria patient while we had afternoon tea in her wealthy grandmother's parlor. My long hair frizzed into an Afro of continental proportions. And the hot shrimp creole her mother prepared felt like burning tar in my tender meat-and-potatoes mouth.

The final blow came when I met her father a few days later. An inveterate angler who to this day manages to fish (ocean, stream, pond, or rain puddle) 365 days a year, he had been down on the gulf when I had arrived, so Nancy had arranged an extended family picnic at Lake Pontchartrain where he would meet us on his way back to New Orleans.

Charles Crawford Henderson arrived in a grayish Chevy wagon and strode right across the grass right in my direction, arms swinging, face lined and burned, a vision of southern manhood, right hand extended. Although I managed the manly grasp, I also noticed my hand looked like a dead whitefish in his reddish brown mitt.

And his very first words to me were, "So, do you fish?"

If it was possible to grow paler than I already was, I'm certain I blanched. "Well, yes, no, I mean I've been fishing, but I'm not really . . ."

He looked angry. "Well, do you hunt?"

"Ummm, no . . ."

Now he looked confused. My throat was clogged, my mind a swamp. Finally I uttered the only thing that made it through the tangles: "Patti and I rode horses over at Audubon Park today."

"Oh." He lit up. "You ride horses?"

"No, not really." I sank in the muck. "It was my first time."

He shook his head and looked haplessly over at Uncle Bruce. "Well, you don't fish, you don't hunt, you don't ride horses—what do you do?"

While looking for a tree to back up against in case I fainted or got attacked, I scurried around behind my glazing eyes desperately searching for some manly conversation to please the old man. A fourth-year college sophomore didn't seem quite impressive enough. A former high school athlete who hadn't run across a highway in at least three years didn't seem to be the key. A bourbon drinker might have been a possibility, but it was too risky.

My mouth opened but nothing came out. The family was leaning in my direction, waiting. Patti's father had his hands on his hips, waiting. I was drowning.

Then from behind, right over my left shoulder like a fairy godmother, came Patti's mother's soft southern voice: "Why, he's a poet, Charles."

His eyes rolled back into his head, and the groan he suppressed might have created a tidal wave on the lake. I don't remember anything after that.

Alone in the guest room bed several hours later, I made plans to pack it all in and race back to New Yawk as fast as I could, my tail between my legs. I lay there muttering to myself in cinematic New Yorkese: *I'm outahere . . . I'm outahere . . . I shoulda just stayed in my own backyard with my own kind . . . I coulda been a contenda. . . .*

But the next morning I was awakened early, had a cup of muddy French Market coffee poured down my throat, and was shuttled into the backseat of the family car before I was lucid enough to tell everyone I was going home. We were already across the Mississippi line when I realized we were headed to Biloxi to meet Patti's grandmother, Eleanor Magruder Sharp. Patti called her Damma.

Damma lived in a little brown bungalow on Lee Street, about a block and a half off the old two-lane U.S. 90 and the Gulf of Mexico. As we pulled into the narrow sandy driveway, Damma was outside with a nearly blind old man named Sam who was supposed to be trimming her rather anorexic-looking hedge. A short grandmotherly woman with a massive tilting pile of white hair on the top of her head and an enormous bosom, she walked right up and grabbed me by the forearm, yanked me down, and gave me a wet kiss.

While she still had me bent over, she turned to Patti and said, "Mmmm, he smells good, this one. I'd keep 'im." Then she added with a wink, "I didn't like the last one. And the old one—what's his name?—was a good boy, but I like this one better. He smells good."

And that was that. She let go and I stood up, a member of the family. Nothing else seemed to matter.

We went inside and she served us her gumbo out of an overflowing soup tureen, a dark pond filling my blue-and-white bowl, fish and oysters and shrimp and okra and whatever else she could find to chop and slice and dump into the witch's brew that transformed me with the first spoonful.

I had never tasted anything so dark and spicy and suggestive of the sensuous bottom of the sea. I understood more with every spoonful what Patti had been talking about all the months I really knew her. I tasted what she tasted. I learned the language. I ate well. I smelled good. I loved her more than ever. Everything was suddenly connected.

And the next day when we drove over to Pascagoula to meet Uncle Jimmy and Aunt Jane (and Covington, Brucie, and Lucie), I even rectified my image a bit with Charles. Weary of pleasant conversation and looking for any excuse to escape the scrutiny of the adults, I offered to shoot hoops with Covington. That's when my future father-in-law found out that I had played on my high school basketball team and decided I wasn't quite as completely worthless as he had assumed.

I had become a *contenda*.

THE WEDDING OF
NORTH AND SOUTH

New York Jews in dark suits, girdles, and frizzy blue hair mingling with New Orleans Episcopalians in white linen suits and breezy countenances and red noses

'Tis opposites—entice—
Deformed Men—ponder Grace
Bright fires—the Blanketless
The Lost—Day's face—
—EMILY DICKINSON

The first sensation that staggers August visitors arriving in New Orleans is the intense, dizzying humidity. Stumbling down the ramps off air-conditioned Delta jets or Greyhound buses, they look like they're going to faint.

The second thing that happens is that their carefully coiffed hairdos blow up like bags of burned microwave popcorn before they even make it out of the airport or bus station.

And so it was for the Levy-Lewis hordes crossing the Mason-Dixon line like Hannibal crossing the Alps to see Sammy's boy Stevie—yes, at twenty-two they still called me Stevie—get married to the—shhhh . . . shiksa—from down south.

New Orleans (pronounced New Orlyuns with the accent on the Or not the Lyuns or Leans) isn't like Florida, where everybody is really from New York. It also isn't some backwater Georgia speed trap off U.S. 95 where so many snowbirds from New York spend a few expensive hours en route to Florida. It isn't like anywhere else in the world. Entering New Orleans is like entering some foreign protectorate.

At the wedding, held in Patti's house in the Garden District, there was no confusion about who belonged to whom. If we had had a theme like some contemporary weddings seem to do, we could have called it Cognitive Dissonance. The natives were breezily dressed in their white linen suits and dresses. They mingled together in bemused, understated casualness, sweating drinks in napkined hands, watching in controlled horror as the invaders schmoozed and schpritzed through the beautiful (*be-yew-tee-ful*, as Aunt Betty used to say) but un-air-conditioned home.

And my people were indeed schmoozing and schpritzing, wrapped in the dark suits and heavy sequined dresses of the neo-traditional bar mitzvah or wedding or twenty-fifth-anniversary affair held at Leonard's on Northern Boulevard. The women's blue hair frizzed into big pelican nests; the men mopped their considerable brows.

There was Uncle Max—the man who defined the plaid-on-plaid-with-argyle-kneesocks look at summer barbecues—with his massive cigar talking at commodities trader Sam Livaday with those broken capillaries highlighting his pale cheekbones and nose. It was clear to anyone walking by that they didn't speak the same language—Max talking like rapid gunfire out of the side of his mouth ("Yaddayaddayaddayaddayadda . . ."); Sam nodding in polite confusion and then slurring out a rather slow but measured generic response designed to fit any social repartee.

And there was Aunt Betty, trapped in her girdle like the rest of my aunts, pinching the cheeks of sophisticated adults who had not had their cheeks pinched since they were knee high to a grasshopper. That warm round face, that wonderfully massive Victorian shelf of a bosom, those unbelievable salamis swinging from her upper arms.

Then there was Patti's great-uncle Charlie, the one who lived alone in his mansion on First Street, drool on his bright yellow tie, wandering around with a confused countenance, no doubt wondering if this was just a Jewish costume rehearsal for Comus; her uncle Bruce drawlin' on about fishin' and shrimpin' and huntin' and crabbin' and, of course, crab bawls and pee-can pies to my best man and official nonoutdoorsman, Richard Gaynor, "one toke over the line, sweet Jesus."

My favorite moment, though, was Uncle Murray handing out his business cards—MURRAY A. LEVY, FIRE ADJUSTER—to all the profoundly bewildered Garden District gentry ("Hey, ya never know . . .") who thought they'd had one bourbon too many and walked into that recurring dream of currency.

And then, of course, there was Patti and me, the living embodiment of love's oxymoronic nature, the yin and yang of earthly constitutions, the Zen paradigm of opposites being twins, stuck on the receiving line for hours on end getting drunker and drunker with each gracious handshake and polite well-wishing—Patti swilling and spilling champagne down the front of her wedding dress, catching the flowers on fire as she lit a cigarette—the two of us leaving the reception for the rest of our lives long before the party was over.

We spent the night in the elegant Royal Orleans Hotel down in the French Quarter, ordered room service fit for the adolescents we were, and watched Hubert Humphrey take the Democratic nomination for president in Chicago.

Everything was perfect—perfectly bizarre—exactly as it should have been. Nothing fit, not even the white linen suit Patti's mother bought for me after seeing the wool suit I'd brought to get married in. Like a deformed man, I pondered grace.

I still do.

FAMOUS ZEN LAST WORDS II

"Let's wait to have a baby until we graduate."

> *Do I contradict myself?*
> *Very well then I contradict myself.*
> —WALT WHITMAN

In late September 1968, three or four weeks after returning from our three-dollars-a-day honeymoon in Wales, London, and Paris, Patti and I threw off the wrinkled sheets of connubial bliss and had our very first serious talk about the future. I mean The Future, as in what we were gonna do when we grew up and got real jobs and car loans and a mortgage and had, like wow, a family.

Far out.

It was a pretty bold concept for two young hippies who had difficulty seeing around the corner of the next weekend. We were then fourth-year sophomores on the unofficial six- or seven-year plan at the University of Wisconsin (enroll a semester, drop a course or two, drop out altogether, re-enroll). Patti was a psychology major with absolutely no interest in becoming a mental health counselor of any kind. I was an English major who thought it would be nice to make a living as a poet. Meanwhile, I was washing dishes at Mama Brava's.

You might easily surmise that we were ill-advised to get married—or even be enrolled in college. At the time, I think every-one we knew, except perhaps a close college friend majoring in psilocybin, was surmising the same thing. But, of course, we were in love, profoundly deaf to the whispered warnings of others, and blinded by desire to any danger signs they planted in the road ahead of us. We went right ahead over the cliff.

So, there we were in Middletown, living in a rental cottage the size of the small room in which I am now writing, arriving late to evening classes, discussing as earnestly as we knew how the one topic we were least knowledgeable in: mature married life.

The career angle was simply too abstract, so we just left that behind with a sort of dumb blind faith (a shrug and a smirk) that things would work out in the end. As Confucius wrote, "It does not matter how slowly you go so long as you do not stop."

Then there was the baby question. On the surface, that was even easier to figure out. It has long been common wisdom that having a baby before you are stable emotionally and economi-cally is a blueprint for marital distress and failure. Both desper-ately trying to be mature, she nodded and I nodded.

We agreed that we would just wait until we were ready. (I'm pretty sure that meant waiting till both had graduated and I was making big money as a poet.) The mere thought of being a fa-ther at my tender age was still a bit bizarre for me—how could I be a father when I was still battling my own? That was the ma-ture, reasoned side of the discussion that evening.

However, there was also a palpable sadness that passed be-tween us at that very reasonable moment. During our brief but wonderfully romantic long-distance courtship (for most of those nine months, I was in Cambridge, Massachusetts, and Patti was in Madison), we had fantasized again and again, as young lovers do, about our future home together: a big white wooden house with wallpapered rooms and porches and porch swings all around set at the edge of a stream in the middle of a lush green meadow, the heartwarming, soulful sounds of twelve kids laughing and ˉˡ◌ᵥᵢₙ◌ in the flowered yard. Yes, twelve kids.

Having both come from small families, the dozen children vision was nothing less than complete and utter fantasy. And actually the fantasy was mostly Patti's, a deeply ingrained sense of destiny that she had had since she was a little girl. I, who had once dreamed of becoming a hermit in Nova Scotia, basically traveled along with her fantasy and eventually even adopted it as my own, no doubt because I loved her more than I had ever loved anyone or anything in the universe—and the vision made her happy. And if she was happy, I was happy. Simple as that.

And it was simply sad to have to acknowledge that we'd have to put off our vision of paradise, at least for a few years.

Which was when Patti looked at me, head tilted and eyes twinkling, and shrugged and smiled and held out that elegant hand for me. I reached over and touched her skin and suddenly loved her in a whole new way. It was like a dream of opening a door you've never seen before and, upon opening it, discovering a wonderful summer porch off your bedroom where you feel more at home than you've ever felt in your life.

And in that moment, holding each other's hand like two children at the brink of the wilderness, we silently agreed that while our life together was already full of questions and contradictions and questionable motives and unbelievably poor decisions, there was no time like the present to be pregnant and have a baby. We felt as large as the universe. We contained multitudes.

2

Zen Pregnancy, Zen Birth

MOON BIRTH

Cael is born; a man walks on the moon

Nothing is born, nothing is destroyed. Away with your dualism, your likes and dislikes. When you have perceived this, you will have mounted the Chariot of the Buddhas.

—HUANG PO

Much to my youthful surprise, the earth-shattering news on July 17, 1969, was not my son's birth.

In the delivery room at St. Mary's Hospital in Madison, Wisconsin, the nurses smiled behind their green masks and the fatherly obstetrician patted Patti on the knee and then shook my shaking hand. But that was it.

There were no heartfelt embraces. No tears. No champagne. This was a birth like any other birth in the obstetrical ward at St. Mary's—and judging by the way everyone scooted out of the delivery room, there was bigger news going on outside.

Out in the corridors it was as still as outer space. I'm not sure what I expected when I puffed up my boyish chest and pushed my way out of the swinging doors, but there were certainly no bands. No fireworks. No reporters from the *Capital Times*.

As I walked down the hall that afternoon peeking into opened rooms I saw what the quiet was all about: patients and staff were all pugged into the airborne Zeniths, and from there into the cosmos, where Neil Armstrong was less than seventy-two hours away from walking on the moon.

Frankly, I have never been much excited by rockets and space travel. The appeal of Superman, Captain Video, and later, Captain Kirk had passed me by like a far-off meteor whizzing above my head as I was looking down at my feet. I always saw life in more earthy—or earthly—terms: the Brooklyn Dodgers, Camp Deerwood, the bounce of a leather basketball, my pal Richard. Later it was Muddy Waters, a green Morgan 4/4, William Carlos Williams, a pitcher of beer, the Vietnam War, Patti. Patti. Patti.

And then there was Cael, purple-faced and mush-headed wailing like a police siren after a grueling twelve-hour labor and delivery. He was a beauty.

After phoning my mother, who did surprise me by crying, I called everyone else I ever knew in my entire life all over the country, but most of them were not home. Then I raced over to the Rathskellar in the Student Union and found a halo-haired boy named Art Ohlman and a few of his friends sitting around a metal table on the shoreline terrace at Lake Mendota. I told them of the miracle of Cael's birth. Art smiled broadly and said his best "Far out!" and gave me a big bear hug, but then there was nothing more to say. He was as far from the experience of young fatherhood as I was from walking on the moon.

And several hours later, Madison growing dark and crickety and the moon beaming through the hospital window, Patti, Cael, and I sat alone in a semiprivate room with the powerful and terrifying knowledge that we had created life—and that life was suddenly here, not coming in nine months or next week or, as it sometimes seemed, eventually coming like some kind of messiah.

He was here, he had a name, crying and suckling on her breast, and in the space of one yowling moment the enormous unencompassable universe was transformed into something as small as the hospital bed where the three of us were huddled together in fearful awe of what Patti had just done.

The next morning before going to the hospital, I stopped at

Rennebohm's Drug Store on State Street for a cup of coffee. On the stool next to mine was a copy of the *Wisconsin State Journal*. The front page was all Apollo 11, as were pages two and three—even the Vietnam War was buried on page four—but I sat there and flipped the noisy sheets until I got way back to the birth announcements, my finger moving down the small print, desperately seeking our names.

Of course, the words and the names weren't there. As I know now, birth announcements are listed a week or weeks after the fact. Still, I was stunned that there was not even a mention of my wife's Artemisian effort to bring new life into the universe or Cael's courageous presence among the newly born. I had witnessed the miracle of the ages right in town, and it seemed nearly as miraculous that the local paper was so focused on a few astronauts soaring off to a dead moon 238,000 miles away from the hospital that they didn't notice the real news.

Two days later, though, on July 20, 1969, Patti and I watched wide-eyed from her hospital room as Neil Armstrong stepped off the landing module and spoke his immediately immortal lines. Everyone cheered in the corridors. Patti cheered. Cael yowled. Even I felt stirred inside by the magnitude of the event, but I was eternally annoyed that the fireworks and bands and corks popping all over the country were for the crew of Apollo 11, not for Patti and Cael.

That evening I sat alone on the rickety pier of our cottage on Lake Kegonsa, sunnies flipping out of the water, and looked up at the moon and understood, perhaps for the first time, just how absurd and wonderful human beings can be.

I dipped my bare feet in the cool water, the moon rippling out beneath the pier, and cheered for all of us: the fireworks and America and Neil Armstrong, but mostly for Cael and Patti, who had given up all dualism and mounted the chariot of the Buddhas.

NO SEX, NO LIES,
NO VIDEOTAPE

Zen facts of pregnant life for fathers

*Certainly nothing is unnatural that is not physically
impossible.*

—RICHARD BRINSLEY SHERIDAN

I know that I should be a little more high-minded about these
things, but as everyone knows, early on in most relationships it's
all about the body. The flesh. Rubbing up against each other in
the dark. The ooooooh. And the aaaaaaaaaaah. The extraordinary capacity for pleasure one experiences through the shared
communion of physical love.

And that's the way it should be. It is, so it should be. Just
as Siddhartha couldn't escape the world by joining a group of
ascetics who lived in the forest and preached the denial of
the self—he had to learn the ways of the body to find his way
to the soul—I believe that sex is one path, among many others, that enables us to achieve true spiritual or transcendent
union with another human being. Carnal knowledge is, after
all, knowledge.

So I knew Patti and Patti knew me—just as it is written in
the Bible. And knowing each other in that way was a lot of fun.
Actually, a whole lot of fun. And educational, too. Although we

were good friends long before we were lovers, I don't think we knew each other very well in our souls.

Frankly, I don't think that makes us any different than most newlyweds or newly somethings. Young couples have sex anywhere, anytime, in any position, and any number of times during any given day. And so it was with us.

Until Cael was conceived. Then the X-rated video of connubial bliss turned to an R (morning sickness, fatigue, language), which was still very nice, but, you know, not quite the spontaneous anywhere, anytime, any which way it had been. And, yes, it all came as a bit of a shock for me; it was difficult to imagine or admit, but her mind was sometimes other places than in bed with me.

I'd say sex maintained an R rating for much of the first trimester, but, unbeknownst to me, there were still deeper and more profound changes awaiting us in the second three months of that pregnancy. Along with some back pain, hormone changes, and a growing connection to and obsession with the tiny life growing in her young body, Patti turned down the heat and led us right (or left) into the realm of PG-13 for the next three months—i.e., a lot more talk than action.

Then, in late April or early May, just as she was making the transition from waltzing sensuously and proudly across campus with her round belly pushed out in front of her to complaining about feeling like a guernsey and waddling (right hand in the small of her back, left hand wiping the sweat from her brow, eyes looking everywhere for a place to sit), our sex life achieved as close to a PG rating as one can get and still be termed marital relations—mostly hand-holding, shoulder rubs, and dreamy internal monologues of how it used to be.

And then, of course, there were the totally celibate G-rated six weeks before and after the birth itself. No more needs to be said about that period.

Considering the most recent findings that young men think of sex every fifteen seconds, over the course of the pregnancy I increasingly had a lot of time to ponder (and grow morose about) Patti's lack of interest in me. And she had an equal amount of time to ponder the pimply adolescent scowl on my face.

Thus, over the surprisingly hilly course of those forty increasingly celibate weeks—and refined over twenty-seven years of marriage and seven full-term pregnancies—I learned nine important Zen facts of pregnant life for husbands:

1. Nine months may be an eternity but it is not a very long time.
2. Extraordinary sex may be sexless.
3. All men are not nearly as irresistible or understanding or sensitive or unique as we think we are—in or out of bed.
4. Absurd as it may sound, a man is not his penis.
5. A man does not die from sexual frustration.
6. A man does not die from leaving his boyhood sexual illusions behind.
7. Pouting is not only unmanly, it gets you nowhere, especially with sex.
8. A man's lust is not self-limiting. Nothing is unnatural that is not physically impossible.
9. Sex, like good wine and deep love, gets better with age.

SEASONS OF BLOOD

*Affirmations of life and love
after two miscarriages*

*The world is impermanent. One should constantly re-
member death.*

— SRI RAMAKRISHNA

Our second-floor apartment on North Newhall Street in Milwaukee was yowling with life: three dogs, two cats, and little
mop-headed Cael, fifteen months old and gearing up his considerable lungs for the ascent into the terrible twos. Life, it may be
said, was full of life. And so was Patti: pregnant, a blossoming
flower for all to see.

Although her mother's untimely death (just a month before
Cael was born) had been a wrenching reminder for all of us
about the terrible and awesome and paradoxical cycle of existence, in that early fall of 1970, while Lake Michigan was growing colder by the day, preparing to transform black water into
white ice, the east side of this overgrown factory town was so
full of blue sky and warm color that you could easily fool yourself into believing that winter would never come.

In the small and worn backyards fronting the alleys, onion
grass still sprouted like hairs on a balding man's head. Even
along the tired and bereft brick foundation walls of the two-

family house where we lived, throngs of chrysanthemums warmed the cold earth. And although the Brewers had recently thrown the sheets over the box seats at County Stadium, the windowless door at Tony's Bar was still held open with a cinder block on sunny afternoons.

Life was good. Damn good. Despite all the calendar-driven evidence to the contrary, everything was ascending, blooming, sparkling, vibrant. That fall I was teaching at a group home for delinquent teenage girls and doing graduate work at the University of Wisconsin-Milwaukee. And with our two-bedroom flat growing smaller by the day, Patti and I started dreaming of buying one of the small charming older homes in the neighborhood. To quote an absolutely awful song from that era, "Everything is beautiful in its own way." And I truly believed it. Everything I saw walking back from the college each day reminded me of the living, breathing embodiment of the eternal, immortal nature of life. (Did I mention that I was an ascending youthful poet?)

So when Patti walked out of the bathroom one evening with worry scribbled across her lovely face, I figured she was concerned about matters more mundane than life and death. Even when she said a few moments later that she was spotting, I remained undaunted; I put my arm around her shoulders and whispered in my most manly warble that everything would be okay. And, of course, I meant it. I felt as invincible as the spring that seemed to be able to leapfrog over the winter that supposedly lay out ahead of us. I *knew* in my heart that everything would be fine. How could it not? When you're young and in love, pregnancy is nothing less than a certain sign that everything is right in the world. We were in tune with nature and nature was about the consummate power of life. We were indomitable.

But nature, we were to discover once again, is not just about life and regeneration, it is also about the inexorable rhythms of existence, including degeneration and death. It is about dark spots on white toilet tissue turning bright red; it is about silent rides up to Whitefish Bay to find that white-coated doctors are as powerless and ignorant as the flannel-shirted crowd in dealing with the inscrutable logic of nature; it is about blood dripping down the inside of alabaster thighs; it is about the lonely wailing after the profoundly quiet passing, walking aimlessly through the incontrovertible streets day after grieving day.

A miscarriage is about one of you mourning a dream and the other grieving what was once real and suddenly is not; it is about turning on a light in our separate corridors of grief and finding that at the end we are all together in our aloneness.

And, some months later, in due time—in due time—it is about healing and falling in love again and getting on with the unfettered hopefulness of life (though with slightly less exuberance this time). It is about planting the seed and making the phone calls and planning the nursery and making yourself believe again in the indomitable power of life. . . .

And then watching hopelessly, hopelessly, angrily, as the dark stains reappear and then turn bright red and begin to flow like a river across a crumbling dam of our most youthful life-affirming assumptions. The very ones you thought you'd left behind the first time around.

The very same ones you've come to rediscover—as if for the first time—when she miraculously grows pregnant again, her eyes bluer than blue, her belly round as fruit. Then you know that it is in the nature of nature to let us know that we are as immortal as we are mere mortals. We die and we do not die.

And so it is also about how fragile we are, and strong; how, as Nietzsche suggested, life will break you, but if it doesn't kill you, it will make you stronger in the places where you've been broken; it is about how we come through tragedy to know in our hearts that we need each other over and over again to withstand the vagaries of this life; it is about how love is the one and only redemptive force.

It is, finally, about how damn good it was to hear fat little Nancy yowling the third time around. It is about how every time I see her, I am reminded of our impermanence on this earth and how I see so suddenly the eternal loving space she occupies in my life. And it is then that I feel most alive.

NOTHING IS TO BLAME

Waxing unpoetic

A poem should not mean but be.
—ARCHIBALD MACLEISH

With each child's birth I wrote a poem. To be kind to myself, which every Zen father should be, I wrote each of the poems out of the gush of loving feeling that accompanied the startling vision of my eternal other releasing a child that I helped create from her extraordinary body into the thin air of this existence.

To be unkind to myself, which every Zen father should also be, I wrote the poems, I've come to see, as a way of stealing a little of the spotlight away from Patti (Hey, look at me!), whose act of creation was so much more profound and magical than anything—anything—I could make or do.

In either case—or, more to the point, in both cases—in reading back through the seven pieces, the poems tell more about my development as a father than they do about birth or anything else, for that matter. I still feel the first (for Cael) as deeply as I do the last (for Elizabeth), though the language of each makes them almost unrecognizable as expressions emerging from the same person.

In the poem for Addie you can see my awakening to the utterly plain, ordinary, earthy nature of the most sublime moment in the universe.

When she was conceived we were living in upstate New York, in a two-hundred-year-old brick home just a mile or so from the craggy base of the Shawangunk Mountains. Just as the rest of the sixties counterculture had gone "back to the land," so had we.

On the property were a barn, a rickety carriage house, a tumbledown chicken coop, and a fenced-in pasture that, at first, felt as big as the Ponderosa back forty. (Later on it miraculously shrunk to a single acre.) In addition to the dogs and cats, we added rabbits and goats and, for good measure, allowed a neighbor's horse to live in the field.

I was writing the great American novel and feeling prematurely wizened by the horrors of Vietnam, the revelations of Watergate, and the act of homesteading (more symbolic than actual) in a place where we didn't know a soul. As naive and idealized as my vision of life still might have been at the time, I was first seeing daily existence in all its raw beauty. With Cael in public school, Nancy in diapers, and dirt under my fingernails, there were no more romantic illusions of how the world should be. No more smoke-filled dreams of utopian existence. No more Age of Aquarius.

As Aaron Neville implored each of us who would listen to him, I wanted nothing more than to "tell it like it is." I felt strong and full of the joy and pain of life I had just seen Patti deliver into the world. The title of the following poem comes from "Why I Laugh When Kai Cries" by Gary Snyder.

Nothing's to blame . . .

Ah Addie,

You made it so quick and sloppy,
your first breath, a squeal, a squeal
between your Mama's thighs, your body
still unborn inside
came gushing out, dripping
with all the mess we have
tucked under skin, hidden
behind closed eyes, wiped
away with fluffy towels. And how funny
you looked, scrawny legs folded up
like a curl to your fat belly
and then stretched
upside down
by your ankles
to drain the muck
from your lungs, the pink
insides of your mouth. What
an unaffectionate word *suction* is,
but how lovely to watch the suctioning,
clearing the canals for the air
that minutes before smelled so antiseptic
and then and now smelling clearly
of you and your Mama clearing the air, ah
Addie, I would have licked you clean. You
wailing your song over shiny gums, tongue
wagging inside, trembling
with the fury of a whole world, 7 pounds
10 ounces of clenched and raging anger
that twice before shook my bones,
shook them like an angry father
full of fright and apologies, which left me

laughing deep in the belly,
deep belly laughing for you, Addie
because it is true, nothing is to blame, after all
the fancy words, it is simply this:
one whole person
turning, squirming, pushing and
sliding naked into this life.
No more. No less. All of a sudden.

Just like that.

BRINGIN' IT ALL BACK HOME

Home-birthing Clover

Observe things as they are and don't pay attention to other people.

—HUANG PO

Giving birth in the late sixties to early seventies wasn't quite the lighthearted experience that Mrs. Brady or Mrs. Nelson or Mrs. Reed led us all to believe it should be. Accompanying the accounts of the joyful births of Cael, Nancy, and Addie, it should also be said that Patti was angry (overwhelmed, uncomfortable, frustrated, humiliated) about the uncompromising, patronizing institutionalism she found in every admissions office and nurses' station and doctored phrase in three different hospitals in two states.

She not only deeply resented having to go from the warmth and comfort of our home and drive to a cold institution while she was in labor, she loathed leaving one baby behind with a baby-sitter while she went away for days to birth another. She hated the senseless and inhumane shave and enema that was at that time standard procedure. She was irate at the internals performed in the middle of contractions. She despised the fact that she had to be rolled on a narrow stretcher from a labor room down the hall to a stark white delivery room while she was in transition. She abhorred the medieval delivery table and those awful stirrups. And she was aghast at the cavalier attitude of the obstetricians who showed up just in time to do an episiotomy, catch the baby, and take credit for all the work.

Of course, it should also be said that beyond all that was deplorable about hospitals, she was thrilled beyond description about birthing her babies.

By 1977, however, she was thirty years old, the mother of three, and felt strong enough and had read enough and knew enough about pregnancy and birth and the arrogant nature of too many obstetricians to make the audacious promise to herself that the next baby would be born at home. And it was audacious; very few women outside of communes in northern California and The Farm in Tennessee were doing home births.

Practically everyone from worried sisters to angry obstetricians to acquaintances who knew us only as Cael's parents said it was the wrong thing to do. Practically everyone said we weren't considering the consequences. Practically everyone said we were being selfish. Practically everyone told us that hospitals had changed and that birthing rooms were every bit like bedrooms, just safer.

Well, she observed things as they were and didn't listen to anyone else. And practically everyone was wrong.

Clover, who was conceived in front of the living room fireplace, was born in our upstairs bedroom on Coffey Lane, with the bumpy plaster walls covered in flowered yellow wallpaper and sunlight pouring in through old poured glass windows.

The day was beautiful, sunny, and warm. In the early stages of labor Patti walked around the property and picked wildflowers for the room, capturing the swooning scent from the big lilac at the corner of the barn. And when her labor grew more intense, we called Patti's friend Cathy Fosnot, who would be her birth attendant, and Herb Weinman, the family GP who, against his own "better judgment," had agreed to monitor the birth. Herb brought his wife, Arlene, along as an assistant; she had never before witnessed a birth, not even her own children's.

It was truly Patti's day. From letting each of us know precisely what she needed—and when—to figuring out the most comfortable position to birth the baby, she was in total charge. We cooked them dinner while Patti labored upstairs; Cathy bathed the kids while I took care of the animals; and later I put the kids to bed with the promise that by the time they woke, they would have a little sister or brother.

I won't go into more pastoral descriptions of the day or the radiance of Patti's presence (she was radiant) or even the unforgettable sensation of catching Clover in my own hands as she emerged into our world (after Herb exchanged places with me soon after she had crowned). Suffice it to say, I still get chills recalling the yellow bedroom and the moment of life and the extraordinary power of the woman who pushed that life into the world.

But what I remember as much as anything else about that day and night was the next morning when Cael, Nancy, and Addie shuffled shyly into the bedroom to see their mother and their new baby sister.

They climbed onto the bed and snuggled in. Patti held each of them—and they held their tiny little sister. And everybody cooed and laughed and made horrible faces when Clover scrunched up her tiny mug and filled up her diaper.

What was so heartwarming for me and Patti was that they clearly didn't feel abandoned and confused, as Nancy and Cael had felt after the earlier births. There was no anger, no manic behavior or saccharine sweetness. They actually seemed to like baby Clover.

And then, because they were little kids and had no more than a five-minute span of concentration—and maybe they got bored and hungry because the baby just lay there like a lump—and also because they knew Patti and the little wrinkly thing weren't going anywhere—I took them downstairs to the kitchen for breakfast. Just like any ordinary morning.

Cael went to school and told everybody that he had a new

sister—and that she was born at home. And when he jumped off the school bus that afternoon, he raced upstairs and discovered that his mother and his baby sister were actually still there, and unleashed a smile that could have melted the polar caps. He went up to see them, funfered around a bit, and then raced down the steps to eat some cookies and go out to play. Just like any other day. As Mike Myers would say as Linda Richman, "No big woop."

And, such as it was, it was the biggest woop of all.

HAVE A CIGAR!

*An apology for the rhetoric of
modern birthing fathers*

*If it were possible to talk to the unborn, one could never
explain to them how it feels to be alive, for life is washed in
the speechless real.*

—JACQUES BARZUN

When Cael was born I was just about as full of myself as my young
wife had been full of baby. I was the first father allowed into the
delivery room at St. Mary's Hospital and was justifiably proud of
myself for coaching Patti through twelve grueling hours of labor.

However, I am thankful that I wasn't listening to me when I
recounted the joys of that first birth as if I were the one in labor.
Shameless is the only word that comes to mind. In fact, with
the first five kids, born between 1969 and 1979, I sprinted out
of the various birthing rooms, purposely without a stash of
cigars, but with an enormous and unabashed arsenal of sensitive
phrases, quietly, insistently announcing the wonder and beauty
of "our" births.

With each, adopting a voice I still do not recognize, I emotionally described how we struggled through the early stages of
labor, how we barely survived transition and then pushed the
baby out in what was certainly the most "beautiful moment of
my life." I'm sure that I always added, "It was a miracle."

It would have to have been a miracle.

Of course, I was not sitting on an inner tube while I spoke, nor had I felt nauseated during the first ninety days of our pregnancy, slept on my back for six months, felt like a guernsey during the last few weeks, had a ten-hour muscle spasm in my belly, endured the dry heaves in transition, or had anyone surgically slice my perineum. Also—as long as I'm telling—I had no real plans of getting up for many of the two, four, six, eight (ad nauseam) feedings because *we* nursed our children.

Frankly, I'm not sure how Patti stood by and maintained a smile as I told practically the whole world how I had done her job. One woman I know has suggested that as men are unaccustomed to finding themselves in supporting roles, the shared birth rhetoric may realistically be considered a veiled attempt to steal the show. I can't disagree.

In my heart, I always knew that there was something wrong with all that talk of sharing—even as I was doing it and incidentally getting complimented for my sensitivity—but it was not until Patti became pregnant with Bay (number six), that I began to feel seriously out of place mentioning our cracked nipples. I was climbing over the rhetorical hill. Or perhaps I was already over the hill at thirty-nine and, like many men my age, just beginning to truly discover my own place in the world. In either case, it was an entirely new experience for one who should have been an old hand at such things.

Over those nine months I grew to understand that I had been neglecting what was truly mine as a father and a man. By denying my rightful place at my wife's side, not in the stirrups, I was cheating myself out of an experience that connected me not only to my own father but ultimately to men of all ages.

I slowly became more aware of my distinctive place in the whole generational process, more painfully aware than ever before of the fragile life growing within my wife's uterus and of my immeasurable responsibility to the woman and child I had touched in my own indelible way.

And I respected that pain as the source of my strength, strutting down Main Street upstate in New Paltz just as my father must have done on 172nd Street in Queens during the early spring of 1946, passing out cigars and blowing smoke. And that was almost like being born. Or being a father for the first time.

3

Zen and the Mindless Little Person in Your Bed

THOSE DREAMS OF FALLING

When three in a bed is not a ménage à trois

> *Reality is where we are from moment to moment.*
> —ROBERT LINSSEN

Picture this: You've just spent the last hour and a quarter (not that you're counting) pacing back and forth across the living room doing the daddy jiggle, a hip-dislocating reverberating great ape walk that men magically acquire with the birth of their first babies: back and forth, back and forth, back and forth, large paw of a hand on that tiny delicate head, milky drool soaking your shirt while you hum an indecipherable version of Bob Marley's *Redemption Song* over and over until the screaming collicky infant is first calmed and then finally falls asleep long enough for you to lift the little doll hand to see if it drops in total dreamy unconsciousness. Finally. Finally.

And then, of course, you had to keep the bump 'n' jiggle going down the hall and into the dark nursery, the air scented with baby oil and a reminiscent dash of ammonia, humming and jiggling all the way to the crib, where you gently pried the little monkey from your shoulder and lowered him what seemed to be three or four or five feet down to the bunny and kitty mattress, careful not to jangle the damn airplane mobile, humming, jiggling, patting, patting, patting more and more softly until you're just patting air and tiptoeing backward like some doofy cartoon character out the door, which you leave open a crack so you can check his breathing every twenty-five minutes later on.

And then you're finally in your own bed, nothing between you and the beautiful naked woman who stole your heart a long time ago, the one who can still scratch your itch and who, by the way, you have not been with (in the biblical sense) for more than two months (not that you're counting the four weeks before the birth when she let you know in no uncertain terms that coitus was no longer in her dictionary and the six weeks afterward when words like episiotomy scars, hemorrhoids, and sore nipples replaced the extraordinary "Mmmmmm" in that same dictionary).

Tonight, however, she has let you know in broadly suggestive terms that the book has been reopened, and the pages are fluttering in the wind from her breathy lips, and you are every bit as excited and lusty and nervous (yes, nervous) as you were when you were fifteen and you were in a constant state of excited, nervous lustiness. And no doubt it's that excitement, coupled with an hour and a quarter of jiggling, that has made it absolutely necessary to run to the bathroom before . . . well, just before, you know . . . but, hey, the baby is finally asleep and the night is still night and there's music in the air. . . .

Unfortunately, in the short time that it took you to stumble to the bathroom, do your business (being careful not to flush and wake the little bugger in the next room), and then do the naked racewalk back to the silky comforts of the marriage bed, the song has miraculously changed from Dylan's *Lay Lady Lay* to Simon and Garfunkel's ode to romantic futility and humiliation, *Cecilia*: When you come back to bed, someone's taken your place. La la la la la.

In fact, he's not only taken your place, he's pressed up against her luscious naked body! And he's sucking on her magnificent breast! And worse still, she looks perfectly content, not

strung tight like the shrieky violin that has recently taken up residence in your head and makes your hair stand straight up with
each draw of the bow.

She smiles at you and blows you a kiss as if to say "This will
only be five minutes, don't lose the mood darling. . . ." So you
slide under the covers and lie down on your official six-centime-
ter slice of the marital bed and wait the five, ten, fifteen, twenty
minutes (not that you're counting) in near frenzied expectation
when you suddenly realize that the slurpy sounds of nursing
have long since stopped and have been replaced by a lilting duet
of rhythmic breaths—and then you look over in complete despair and see that little Oedipus and his mother are fast asleep.

And in that instant all those visions of bacchanalian lovemak-
ing that have sustained and kept you edgy lo these many weeks
fall into the trash heap of another cold, lonely night full of
dreams of falling. Falling out of windows. Falling off cliffs.
Falling from the back of speeding trains.

Only this night the dream is not really a dream at all. You
have fallen—out of bed. In the final act of domination, Little Big
Oed, who is fully sated with breast nectar, has scooted around
sideways on the mattress, pressed his stubby but steel-like toes
into your ribs, and pushed you out onto the floor.

I almost wish there were something to say that would enable
new fathers to avoid the inevitable frustration and humiliation
that surely awaits them, but as the man says, "Reality is where we
are from moment to moment." And the reality is that life is
never the same after a baby alters the symmetry of love.

Accept it and move on to the next reality. Sex returns—in
many ways more deeply satisfying than it was before—but you'll
never again be totally alone in bed with your one and only—
even if the door's locked and the children are asleep (or grown
and out of the house).

WHEN "IT" FINALLY
OCCURRED TO ME

The "withness" of the first night home

> We have no right to assume that any physical laws exist, or
> if they existed up to now, that they will continue to exist
> in a similar manner in the future.
>
> —MAX PLANCK

My guess is that Patti grew up gradually over the nine months
she was pregnant with Cael. The profound changes to a woman's
psyche that must by nature go along with a life stirring within
her body must also bring with them an extraordinary sense of
the "withness of the body," to quote Alfred North Whitehead,
and a deep enduring awareness of one's connection to the ebb
and flow of the universe.

Frankly, I didn't know much about "withness" or connection or even that deplorable word *maturity*, primarily because as
a male I spent those same nine months in the same boyish
hormone-driven heroic ("Bottom of the ninth, bases loaded,
Lewis comes to bat . . .") fog that I'd spent the previous twenty-
two years. I was still a kid. I was not only witless, I was withless.

So while Patti was gearing herself up mentally, spiritually,
and physically for the impending, if idealized, visions of birth
and life with an infant, I don't think I was working on any vision
at all. I think I just assumed that after the baby was born, every-

thing would pretty much return to normal: we'd stay up till the early hours of the morning, sleep till noon, go to afternoon classes, party, work when absolutely necessary, rock 'n' roll. If there were any visions rattling around in my hairball of a head, they might only have been about how cool it was going to be to have a little guy in OshKosh overalls, and a blue Brooklyn Dodgers cap and a pint-size Rawlings glove on his tiny hand.

I do remember noticing small but significant changes early on in the pregnancy (besides the watermelon that was turning her belly button from an innie to an outie), like the strange motherly voice I sometimes heard on the phone—and her newly acquired propensity to be on time to appointments—and, most shocking of all, her sudden need for more than three hours' sleep a night. But I also remember thinking that they were temporary aberrations and would disappear as soon as the nine months were up.

And through the next few months of agonizing crib and layette shopping (and doll-size clothes scattered around the house and doctors' appointments and Lamaze classes and, of course, that enormous protrusion between the two of us as I tried valiantly to carry on a sex life), all of which should have alerted me to the fact that my life was never going to be the same again, I'm pretty sure that I remained clueless.

Withless. Even on that spring morning when we were rushing to get to classes on time and she glanced disparagingly down at our two-seater British racing green P1800 into which she had to drop her not inconsiderable girth—and from which she would later on extract herself.

"What?" I asked.

She glowered at me like I was a dithering child. "We need a new car, Steven . . . one that has a backseat and is more than six inches off the ground."

I looked over at the two-seater, a real honey of a Swedish automobile when Swedish cars were still fun to drive, and wondered if it was financially possible to put the 1800 up on blocks and get an old clunker until she came back to her senses. As I said, clueless.

So, it was a stunning moment for me the night after the morning we brought Cael home from the hospital (in our brand-new used station wagon!). We were sitting on the floor—just the three of us where there had only been two just a few days before—in the bare living room of the cottage on Lake Kegonsa, crickets filling the spaces of the warm night outside, water lapping at the shore, both of just staring at this marvelous wailing producer of poop, when it finally occurred to me that I was his father. His Dad. The Old Man. Daddy. Pops. Moneybags. The Doofus Hiding in the Bathroom. The Ride Home from the Dance. And I would never again be the same innocent and childish and footloose and irresponsible and ignorant hipster that I had always aspired to be.

Which is when I turned to Patti in a mild sweat and said, "Let's run into town and get something to eat." It had been common for us in those days—especially as the pregnancy wore on and Patti grew increasingly ravenous—to leave the lake at all sorts of bizarre hours to search for doughnuts in twenty-four-hour places in Madison.

Patti looked at me like I was crazy. "It's almost midnight and I just got him to sleep. I'm completely exhausted. Let's go to bed."

It was as if the avenging angel had swooped down on Stoughton, Wisconsin, and lifted the gummy veil of childhood from my eyes: out ahead lay diapers, two a.m. feedings, baby-sitters, work, health insurance, nursery school, career, middle-school chorus concerts, college tuition, thinning hair, and a paunch. Tea and cookies at eleven o'clock each night. Sansabelt slacks. A condo in Florida. Eternity.

And no more three a.m. doughnuts.

When Patti and Cael fell asleep in our bed soon thereafter, I walked barefoot to the lake and sat down at the edge of the rickety dock, feet dangling in the dark water. I felt old, more deeply tired than I'd known possible at the early hour of one a.m., heavier in spirit than ever before in my young life. I used to think I could walk on water. On that night, a few days after men had walked on the moon, I realized that if I eased myself off the dock, I would slip into the black lake and sink like a stone all the way down to the muck at the bottom.

And that night the water felt cool on my hot skin, my toes pushing off from the muck and my body rising to the moonlit surface and floating off into an extraordinary new life.

CIRCUMCISIO

Some thoughts on circumcision

> *Do not seek to follow in the footsteps of the men of old;*
> *seek what they sought.*
>
> —MATSUO BASHŌ

In 1979 when Danny was born and routinely circumcised by the doctor, Patti took one look at the painful lesion on his tiny penis and swore tearfully that if we *ever* had another boy she would never again allow such a cruel and barbaric mutilation of one of her babies. There was no medical reason for it.

Although reluctant to agree, for reasons still not perfectly clear to me, I nodded sympathetically—and looked away. In truth, I believed it was a nonissue. Danny was our fifth child—and supposed to be our last.

Despite the screaming, the red raw tip of his penis, and a worrisome infection that followed, the fat baby boy eventually healed, and the painful experience was replaced by the joys and anxieties of watching a young child grow. And by 1984 when he entered kindergarten, circumcision was as far from our thoughts as the idea of having a sixth child.

Which is all we were thinking about after watching Danny take that giant step up to the school bus—and we walked back into an empty house. So, in February of 1985 when Patti was six weeks pregnant, the issue instantly became relevant again.

Patti was quick to recall the painful memories of Danny's first few days of life. And I agreed right away that we should talk it over. Sometime. What can you say about something that feels so wrong and so right at the same time?

I tried almost nightly to express my confusion, but every time I opened my mouth, the voices of some angry old men took up residency in my vocal cords and shouted me down. Then one evening I closed my eyes to all the shouting, hoping to visualize a transcendent solution—or something—and when I opened them again Clover was standing in front of me. The resolution.

At that hopeful moment I convinced myself that we were going to have a girl, and as winter turned grudgingly into spring and spring hesitantly into summer I parlayed that resolution into nearly six months of silence on the subject.

In early September, however, when the midwife of our "refresher" Lamaze group wrote CIRCUMCISION on the board, I knew that the comfortingly discomforting silence had come to an end. And after she finished a rather compelling argument against what she called a "cosmetic procedure with significant medical risks associated with it," Patti turned my way as if to say "Well?"

On the ride home there was nothing but silence as I drove down the dark country roads trying to find my voice amid all the shouting going on in my brain. When I was finally able to utter some sounds, I hesitantly told her that it troubled me deeply that the baby—if it was a boy and I was sure it wasn't—would look different from me, his two older brothers, and the vast majority of boys at school. I admitted that even though I had not attended services since I was thirteen, I still felt that it would be a betrayal to go against what has been done to Jewish baby boys for thousands of years. I was concerned that my parents would not understand. As time went on and the gas gauge neared empty, I even admitted, somewhat sheepishly, that I preferred the way circumcised penises look. However, none of those reasons felt exactly right.

Later that evening, disrupting an awkward silence that had lasted for hours, I told Patti the other truth: that despite my obvious wish to avoid the subject altogether, as the father, the burden of the decision should be more mine than hers. It would be me with whom he would have to contend to establish his own identity as a man.

I expected a serious rebuttal—Patti is a strong, self-willed person—but after some private thought of her own she reluctantly agreed, reminding me again of the screams and the raw lesion and the dangerous infection. I nodded.

Had I been totally honest that evening, however, I would have admitted that I knew that the right thing to do was to leave the foreskin intact but that the right thing for me was to have him circumcised. But I could not utter the words. All I could do was hope we would have a girl.

On October 6, Bay Steven was born. It was a wonderful birth; his three sisters, one brother, an aunt, his godmother, and I were all in the birthing room as he emerged into our world. My joy was as pure as I had ever experienced at any birth.

I waited, of course, until the last possible moment to admit to myself and to Patti that I had (long, long ago) decided to follow the old men. On the evening of the second day of his life, I chose circumcision for my infant son.

By the time I arrived at the hospital the next morning, it had already been done. Patti was teary and angry. Bay was crying. When I lifted the small gauze, his tiny penis was red and painfully raw. And for what? The old men who tell that circumcision is a sign of initiation into the community?

There was nothing to do but hold my baby, to accept his pain as my own and welcome him into the confusing community of men, boys all of us, following our fathers' giant footprints in the sand. That night, as I rocked him back and forth, I thought ahead to his days in the tangled woods with his best pals . . . to his afternoons in damp locker rooms with friends and enemies ... to the hazy light of hanging out on street corners with the guys ... to the quiet darkness of sitting in a rocker with his own son. That night I understood that the old men were not wrong, but they were not right. Initiation happens every day of a boy's life when we seek what they sought.

BAYOU GRACE

*Enduring the biggest fright
in a parent's life*

Zen is simply a voice crying "Wake up! Wake up!"
—MAHA STHAVIRA SANGHARAKSHITA

On top of Patti's cluttered dresser is the swirling ultrasound Polaroid taken at the amniocentesis. I don't remember the details of that day, only the sense of well-being I felt driving away from the clinic in New Haven. Of course I had doubts about being a father for the seventh time, but as I had always harbored a feeling in the depths of my soul that we were somehow watched over, I felt in my bones that my family would *always* be protected from anything too painful to endure.

A few weeks later, a genetic counselor called to say the baby was fine. "Perfect," I said to Patti, despite the fact that this was already not a perfect pregnancy. At nearly forty-two, Patti was tired and nauseous much of the time, not quite as resilient as she had been at twenty-two with Cael or at thirty-two with Danny. And to my surprise, the older kids were not exactly thrilled with the idea of another sibling squeezing into our crowded den. At two, Bay was ignorantly blissful, but Danny and Clover, then eight and ten, were concerned about new room arrangements;

Addie, twelve, felt displaced—again; Nancy, fourteen and long past thinking her parents had any self-control, shrugged; and Cael, eighteen, was simply embarrassed. "Oh no!" he blurted out when I called him at college.

Nothing could rock my confidence, though. After six kids nothing could surprise us. Toxemia, labor, hospital birth, home birth, circumcision, colic, sleepless nights, croup, sibling rivalry, and more—we'd been through it all.

So when Elizabeth Bayou-Grace arrived on a warm May day, I imagined her born into a state of grace, cradled by the rippling waters of a bayou in my wife's native Louisiana. She was a gorgeous baby. In fact, everything seemed so right with the world that when the pediatrician detected a condition called congenital hip dysplasia—dislocated hips—I was rather cavalier about it, even as I watched her fitted into a harness that held her knees up to her belly like a frog. I was thankful it was not worse, my optimism rising with the temperature through the summer visits to a specialist at the Hospital for Joint Diseases in New York City.

The fall was a rainy one, however, and the simple joint problem seemed quickly to skid out of our shaky control. First the news that the harness didn't work—both hips were still out of joint—then the frustrating cancellation of several diagnostic tests because of a suspicious low-grade infection. And then, so suddenly it seemed, the soft measured voice of a pediatrician saying to my unbelieving soul that the blood tests indicated a problem totally unrelated to the hip disease: perhaps acute lymphocytic leukemia. He could not confirm it, though.

Through two decades of dark nights in emergency rooms, holding desperately feverish or injured children in my arms, I had never known the helplessness or terror—or betrayal—I felt when I heard those words. I began to wonder how I ever could have seen the world with such certainty.

As the rain turned to snow and ice outside, it was recommended that we move along on the joint problems again and keep a close watch on her blood levels. Elizabeth was placed in traction and was to stay that way for two weeks. Patti warned me on the phone about what to expect when I arrived at the hospital, but how do you prepare yourself to see a beautiful and innocent five-month-old baby flat on her back with her little legs separated and strapped to a pulley-and-weight apparatus attached to the top of a metal crib? I had to step out in the hall to catch my teary breath when my heroic wife climbed up into the crib and leaned bare-breasted over Elizabeth so the wailing baby could nurse.

This was definitely not the way it was supposed to be. During the next two weeks, Patti spent twenty-four hours a day in a cramped hospital room entertaining our frustrated baby and I put nearly three thousand grueling miles on the car commuting between our upstate home, work, and the hospital.

Along the way my older children kept me from skidding off into despair; Nancy, Addie, Clover, and Danny provided mothering and fathering for Bay (and each other) during the many hours I was away; Cael called often from college; and we combined weekend trips to the zoo and the Moscow Circus with visits to the hospital armed with balloons, stuffed animals, and drawings the kids made. Soon the sterile hospital room began to take on some of the warm semblance of home. And Elizabeth's smiling good nature through her ordeal made us all feel as if things were going our way again.

They were not. The traction failed to keep her hips in place, and she was sent directly from X ray to surgery. Hours and hours later when our little baby returned dazed and hurting from recovery, the needle marks, bruises, and horrid incisions we saw provided final proof to me that the protection I had once imagined had never existed at all.

On the way home from the hospital that night, I pulled off the road, laid my forehead on the wheel, and wept as I had not wept since I was Danny's age. I had always thought my most important job as a father was to protect my family from harm, but sitting alone in that cold car, I realized how powerless I was to stop her pain or the cancer. I had no claims on special treatment, no matter what I did or who I knew or how loud I raised my voice in protest.

I felt as forlorn as little Bay, who woke each morning with the same question: "Is Mommy home yet?" And the older kids, weary of worrying, eating at neighbors' homes, baby-sitting and begging rides, began to withdraw from the daily soap opera behind their closed bedroom doors. The eagerly awaited Christmas was approaching, but I walked through the big house shivering in cold pockets of silence.

In retrospect, I think Elizabeth and Patti came home just in time to save us all. As much as they yearned to be surrounded again by family, dogs, cats, ducks, and thirty acres of red and gold fallen leaves, we needed a mother and baby to hold us together. Invigorated by their presence, we put our energies into creating accommodations for a baby in a bulky body cast that went from her armpits to her ankles: car beds out of wicker dog beds, car seats created by sawing away the sides of standard restraints, and a high chair cut out of a butcher-block table on wheels. We decorated for her first Christmas.

The girls often took Elizabeth into their rooms as they talked on the phone or did homework. Danny read books to her, and Bay hovered around his baby sister as if she were his best friend. And most amazing was Elizabeth, who woke singing each morning, actually learning to creep and even climb in the heavy cast by using her small hands to grasp the rug or a chair or a leg and hoist herself along.

The baby who was the focus of my most desolate fear made Christmas '88 as clamorous and wonderful as any in memory. We sat her in the butcher-block high chair and she giggled and squealed through the entire high-voltage morning, paper and ribbons flying everywhere, unaware and unconcerned that her ordeal was not over. At all.

From this vantage point seven years later, I know she had much more ahead of her: another hip operation, more excruciating blood tests, the exhilarating news that she did not have leukemia, the icy disappointment of learning that after all she'd been through, only one hip was in place and she would be confined for more than three years to a heavy brace that held her legs wide apart, her feet in a virtual plié. I know now that the joints would never heal perfectly and that physical therapy would become a way of life.

Yet the baby who lit up that cold Christmas in 1988 eventually got up on her haunches and started crawling in '89; and from there climbed up on Bay's scooter and, using her feet like flippers, began dashing recklessly around the house. Scooting, bumping down stairs, hitching rides on sore hips, or directing us with a vocabulary born of necessity, she became a lesson to all about getting around in an unsteady world.

By Christmas 1990, she actually walked in her brace across the festive living room to the cheers and tears of her screaming family. And in January 1992, Elizabeth Bayou-Grace walked into nursery school without a brace. It was not just a great day. It was a miracle, especially to me, who once let ordinary miracles pass me by.

So as Christmas approaches this year, the energy levels wavering near the paternal red line, it's no surprise that at the center of the frenzy of anticipation here is a seven-year-old who still runs rather unsteadily yet provides enough of a surge to light the densely ornamented spruce in the corner. She has indeed become the spirit of Christmas in our home, the baby who leads us to accept our fragile places in this world without assumptions. A healthy reminder to her father, in this snowy, slippery world, to "Wake up! Wake up!"

ZEN IN THE ARTLESSNESS OF GIVING NAMES, PART I

What's in a name? That which we call a rose
By any other name would smell as sweet.
—SHAKESPEARE

On May 14, 1979, while sitting or, more precisely, squatting on my lap at the edge of our four-poster bed, Patti let forth an archetypally mammoth groan and pushed out one fat little baby boy between her spread thighs, squishy and howling and altogether rather cute despite his bald head.

Patti's sister Leigh was there with us. So was her friend Kitty. And so was Dr. Wooten, home birth doc from the famed Woodstock (where in keeping with the Zen-ness of this book the Woodstock festival was not held). The doctor was kneeling on the rug dressed in an orange jumpsuit. He caught the baby in his sure hands just as the little guy felt the first forces of gravity in his young life. It was all pretty extraordinary.

And, yes, pretty ordinary, too. A simple holy moment. As Milwaukee poet James Hazard writes: "It is an ordinary thing to be holy. We do such extraordinary things not to be." And so it was.

Ordinary, that is. Cael, who was ten at the time, was pretty excited the next morning about finally having a brother after all those sisters, but probably no more so than about the fact that it was Saturday and he didn't have school. However, Nancy and Addie, six and four respectively, in their footed pajamas, thought it was absolutely terrific to have a real live doll baby in the house. And Clover, at two, was clueless but quite happy that her mama was there just like she was there every morning of her life. That was it, though. Life went on unimpeded.

The baby who had been inside her mother for so long was now outside. Simple as that. Suddenly—and generally uneventfully—we went from six to seven in the family. The house was as homey and messy as it had always been. Emma the dog rolled over on her back and begged shamelessly for a scratch. The goats needed feeding. The grass needed mowing. Everything was fine and dandy—and ordinary.

Until Nancy and Cael realized that we hadn't named the little orangutan. Then all hell broke loose.

Frankly, I don't know how we made it forty weeks without figuring out an official name for the new baby, but as you might have gathered by now, we're a little laid-back about some things in our family. We did choose several names for both sexes that each of us liked. It just turned out that we never agreed on the precise one.

And then so suddenly he was born. I figured that it might be a neat idea to try out a few names for the first few days and see how they fit—sort of like a thirty-day free home trial. Patti actually liked the idea.

The kids, however, thought we had lost our marbles. On Sunday, the day after the birth, they were horrified at their parents' blatant irresponsibility. They implored us to give "it" a name.

And early Monday morning when the tubby little muffin still didn't have a real name, they were on the verge of reporting us to the authorities for dereliction of parental duty. "He needs a name!" Cael burst out self-righteously over his oatmeal, sounding a lot like my father.

"How could you not name him?" Nancy snarled, dripping cereal and contempt at our immaturity. As the only truly organized person in the family, she's never been able to abide our messes.

"Yeah," added Addie, our little bulldozer who always spoke the truth. "How are they gonna go to school and tell everybody?"

Ah, we realized, that's the essence of the problem. They were far less concerned about the poor nameless baby than about having to show up at school and admit that their parents were classless jerks. And the problem thus unfurled, Cael forged right ahead with my father's patented either/or stance on life. "We can't go to school and tell everybody that our parents didn't get it together to give our new brother a name." He scrunched up his nose and glared at us. "Either he gets a name or we stay home!"

"Yeah," piped in Nancy, who wasn't sure that this was going to work. "A person needs a name!"

"Yeah," said Addie, who wasn't going to school that day anyway.

Patti and I don't normally take well to being extorted by our children—see the chapter on Zen spanking—but in this instance I admit we understood their abject humiliation and shame. Reasonable or not, it would be embarrassing to have to tell everyone that your parents couldn't figure out a name for your new baby brother more than two days after he was born. The jokes would never end.

So, just before Nancy and Cael walked out the kitchen door that morning, the fat little baby boy got called Daniel Clay Lewis. (Just for the record, there is no significance, personal or otherwise, to either name, and furthermore, we had no idea at the time about Daniel Day Lewis.) They all agreed that they liked that, though I'm sure we could have called him Rin Tin Tin and it would have been all right.

But it was even better than that; it was a regular name, not something weird like Cael or Clover or Adelyn. It was Danny, an all-American name that you could bring to school and not have to hear snorts or snickers or howls.

And he smelled very sweet.

ZEN IN THE ARTLESSNESS
OF GIVING NAMES, PART II

*Our names are the light that glows on the sea waves at
night and then dies without leaving a signature.*
—RABINDRANATH TAGORE

Of course, that was not the end of the issue when Danny finally
got his name. One thing that you learn early and well in a large
family is that nothing is ever simple.

Saddled with a father who for reasons beyond their understanding (and my own) rarely calls his children by the names
inked on their birth certificates, they waited expectantly to hear
what Danny really would be called.

At the time that Danny was born, for example, I was calling
Clover Poochie, which was short for the unwieldy Perchmont
Robert Haldanish. Don't ask why. Zen names are beyond under-
standing. And since that time she's had a wide variety of aliases,
from the pithy Flodunkus to the more je-ne-sais-quoi Florky-
Dorky (or its derivative Flumkin-Dumkin) to the stately Foofie.

Honestly, I don't know. She responds to any of them, though.

And, of course, Clover is not the only one with unusual tags.
Cael is Bubba, but he was Ralph Barco for years. Nancy has
evolved to The Turtle from previous incarnations as Puppy Turtle,

Turkey Puddle, The Scooper, and Woopy Woop for a Full Year till She's Full Grown (which I eventually shortened to Wooper). Addie has worn, among several other monikers, Aderlwyn Yacht, Yetso Yurt, YD, The Bulldozer, and most recently Al-Edward, or Edward for short. Danny, who was Graybadge and E-Man (Encyclopedia Man) and Danzek and Dansak and most recently Darzulu or Zule, is now Donald. Yes, Donald.

Things got simplified with the last two. Maybe I'm just getting old, but the names fit so well, I've just never had the need to transform them again. Bay is The Boofer, first, last, and always. He couldn't be anything else. And Elizabeth Bayou-Grace has been simply (and, I believe, rather elegantly) Bishy for all seven years of her life.

It's been with a mixture of horror and an odd sort of endearment that the children abide my quirks. I can tell you, though, that in that big family stock-in-trade of calling children by their sisters' and brothers' names—"Hey, um, Nancy, Addie, Clover, Danny, whatever your name is, please turn off the light."—I never trip over the private names, the ones destined to be recalled in embarrassed whispers when the children are grown with children of their own and reflecting back on their lost youth.

Yes, everything comes and goes, even names, like the light sparkling off the sea waves at night. They grab our attention, they lap at the sides of the hull, but they are not who we are, except to the one who calls us in the dark. Maybe then.

THE ZEN OF
DIAPER DUNKING

*There is a proper way to swish
cloth diapers in a toilet*

The Way is Not a Way.
—GARY SNYDER

I'm no shirker. I changed diapers for more than twenty-one years. Seven kids and a lot of dirty bottoms later, I'm pretty much of an expert in the field. In fact, estimating ten thousand diapers per child from birth to toilet training, Patti and I have probably lifted more bottoms than the entire academy of plastic surgeons.

Back in the old hippie days, when the earth seemed big enough to absorb all the world's garbage without so much as a queasy equator, we used the first varieties of paper diapers. They were pretty primitive by today's standards—rather bulky, they had no elastic and no tabs, didn't absorb well, and didn't hold much in—but they were disposable. And even more important, you didn't have to dip them in the toilet, a truly awful job, certain to cause most grown men great grief. We loved disposables, especially when we were traveling. If they weren't so costly (relative to washing our own cloth diapers at the laundromat) we would have used them all the time.

As the years, family income, and number of children mounted

proportionally, however, we began to use paper diapers exclusively. In the seventies, when "single-use disposables" achieved space-age performance and convenience, we became a major supplier of solid waste to the local landfill. I estimate that twelve years must have passed between the time that I dunked (and dunked and dunked and dunked) my last cloth diaper in a toilet and the day Bay (number six) was born into the world's burgeoning awareness of a garbage crisis.

The facts about the world's solid waste problems—and the single-use diaper's role in filling and contaminating earth and water—are well known by now. I won't drive down that road. My point is that after Patti and I decided to return to cloth diapers as one specific solution to try to keep the world spinning cleanly on its axis, I was suddenly back dipping diapers in the toilet.

And whining in a most unbecoming fashion.

Frankly, I didn't want to be in my sophisticated forties and be seen hunched over the porcelain throne holding the one clean corner of a messy diaper between thumb and forefinger, dunking and swishing (dunking and swishing), wondering how I was going to wring out the excess water when I was finished without getting my hands dirty. I'll admit that on a few occasions I actually dropped the diaper in the toilet and walked out, leaving the awful job to the next unsuspecting person who stumbled into the bathroom to, of all things, go to the bathroom.

I yearned pathetically for the old disposable way of life. Being an English teacher, I might even have moaned something like "Something is rotten in the state of Denmark" when that old familiar odor wafted its way across the room. I pined out loud that life was already messy enough, hoping that someone would come to my rescue and do the dirty deed.

And as the months went on and I continued to try to weasel out of changing Bay's diapers, my wife and kids began to look at me with disdain. Nancy's scowl reminded me of Claudius's words about the melancholy Hamlet of the same rotten Denmark: "T'is unmanly grief."

And so it was. Though the Bard's words reflect much weightier matters than a load in an infant's pants, the meaning is the same for all fathers: whether it's revenge for your father's murder or wiping the schmutz off your baby's bottom or cleaning up the environment, there is a proper way for us to approach the unpleasant realities of fatherhood.

Unfortunately, there is no way to wring out a sopping wet diaper with the tips of two fingers on one hand. I've tried. You have to get your hands dirty. The art of it is, as mothers have always known, that there is no art.

Diaper dunking is done mindlessly. You take a deep breath and plunge right in. Dunk and swish until the diaper has nothing stuck to it and then, without even a second's pause, grab it with both mitts, fold it once, wring the sucker out, and slam-dunk it into the diaper pail. That's it.

And don't forget to wash your hands—and keep your nails short.

4

The Suchness of Life with Toddlers

SURVIVING THE
TERRIBLE TWOS

A road map for the lost and weary

'Tis as manlike to bear extremities as godlike to forgive.
—JOHN FORD

Included with the basket of diapers and lotions that are sent home with every infant from every maternity ward in the country should be a three-year supply of fortune cookies with two separate messages inside:

> Throw away all those how-to-parent books. Just keep in mind who is the parent and who is the child. Nothing else matters.

> Every two-year-old exists solely to test your sanity. Be as patient as the universe but don't be quite so limitless.

Two-year-olds are really cute. Really cute. Moppy hair and OshKosh overalls and brand-new stubby teeth and short chunky little legs and sweet little raspy voices that call you Daddy.

They're so cute that when they stand in front of you, hands on nonexistent hips, bellowing out an adamant NO!, we actually laugh. They're so cute, in fact, that I think there's a Darwinian survival mechanism involved in their cuteness. Otherwise they'd never survive.

They're cute, but they're bad.

So, there's no irony or transcendent double entendre in the designation terrible twos. Two-year-olds are terrible. You've seen them in the grocery stores, in the malls, in churches and synagogues, in your own living rooms. They touch everything they can reach; they break everything they can touch; and they throw tantrums every single time they can't reach something they want to touch and break.

And they say NO! to everything in the universe.

I'll skip the psychobabble about independence and the inner child and self-esteem and separation anxiety and gender identification. Let's just define the two forms of a tantrum: *home* and *away*, just like in sports.

A *home* tantrum involves lying on the floor and kicking your legs and screaming (often screeching) and sometimes holding your breath until you turn an odd shade of blue or gray, depending on your cultural diversity factor. For most adults it's a no-brainer. Any reasonable parent will simply walk out of the room, thus ending the tantrum. A tantrum, like a tango, takes two people.

Just a side note: if you think that you can outyell or out-tantrum a two-year-old having a tantrum, give it up. You can't. As the saying might go, any self-respecting two-year-old can tantrum any grown man under the table, which is where your wife will find you when she gets home, babbling to yourself like Tony Perkins in *Psycho*.

And here's another one: trying to reason with a toddler having a tantrum is such an absurd concept, it doesn't even warrant further comment.

An *away* or public tantrum is very different. It involves being sprawled on the floor of the supermarket or the mall or a family friend's living room and kicking your legs and screeching and sometimes holding your breath, just like a home tantrum. The difference, of course, is that there are adults besides your parents around to scoff and snicker at the scene.

Most parents are painfully embarrassed at the sight of their kids writhing on the filthy floor, and try to make lame explanations to the other adults gawking on in smug disapproval like "I've never seen her like this" or "He must be coming down with something." Then they try to get their unruly children to stop and behave, either by making unenforceable threats ("The store manager is going to call the police") or talking in that sickly sweet voice that you hear on PBS kids' shows. Either way the parent loses. The kid's got a rapt audience and the harried parent's complete and undivided attention—and the tantrum won't stop until she or he has your power of attorney.

I hate to be so definitive—and so traditional—and so un-Zen—but there are only two possible courses of action to save you from abject humiliation—and along the way maybe even do your kid a favor. The first is to walk away, just like you do at home. (You might say something patently parental like "I don't listen when you act that way" if that makes you feel better. It actually doesn't matter what you say.)

If walking away is not possible—for instance, when your tot is disturbing other people, like in a movie (been there) or a restaurant (seen it) or a friend's living room (done it)—then Plan Two goes into effect. You simply pick 'em up, turn 'em sideways, and hoist 'em onto your better hip (head forward, kicking feet back) and remove 'em from civilized society. A car is a good holding tank. So is a park or a backyard in warm weather. Two-year-olds calm down very quickly when they realize a tantram is not working.

Then they get remorseful—and cute: tear-stained faces, wet matted hair, and grubby little paws up in the air begging a hug. The sight is so cute that you are instantly filled with tenderness, hugging them as if they've been lost for days and just been found. And in that wonderfully warm (and probably wet) moment you wonder how it's possible that you were so furious with them just a few moments ago.

Which is precisely when, of course, the little imp smirks over your shoulder, knowing she has just earned the upper hand for the next tantrum coming down the pike.

WHAT IS THE SOUND OF ONE HAND SPANKING?

Some non-PC thoughts on discipline

> *A master, Gutei, whenever he was asked the meaning of Zen, lifted his index finger. That was all. Another kicked a ball. Still another slapped the inquirer.*
>
> —HUSTON SMITH

When it comes to the more sticky realms of parenting, like whether it's okay to spank the little urchin for crimes against parental humanity, I generally turn to my wife as guide or guru. She knows more than I do.

I know I'm not supposed to say that, but it's true. Given the undeniable fact that mothers and babies share organ systems for forty of the most meaningful weeks in a person's life, it's reasonable to conclude that most mothers know more about children than most fathers, which does not necessarily mean that they make better parents. They just know more intuitively. Patti certainly does—plus she's not really the enigmatic type, which is a great help for me when I find myself in an ethical or moral morass about things like the spanking issue.

Her sphinxlike advice? "Swat 'em when they need it."

She draws most of her good knowledge from observing animals. Animals, she says, don't ponder correct behavior, they live it, drawing on eons of knowledge of survival. In Zen terms they know what is—they have "isness."

In contrast, far too many childcare experts (with M.D.s and Ph.D.s dangling off their names like price tags off sale rack clothing), deal only with what *should* be. Despite those same eons of evidence that human beings are aggressively territorial, they believe we *should* be able to live meat-free as well as aggression-free. Karen Horney, my favorite social theorist, called it "The tyranny of the shoulds" and suggested that the should system is directly responsible for the formation of self-destructive behavior patterns in children and other living things.

Anyway, Patti says it's okay to spank if the situation warrants it and you don't leave any marks. She says "Look at how dogs and cats (and monkeys and lions) handle their babies when they get obnoxious." They growl or snarl first and then out comes the paw and they swat 'em. Not hard enough to hurt, but hard enough to let 'em know they've been scolded. And the pups or kittens pick themselves up and go away—presumably without any psychological scars or damage to their self-esteem.

The central fact of life with toddlers is that it is virtually impossible to communicate via pure language with them. If you think men and women speak different dialects—and it's pretty clear that we do (read Deborah Tannen's *You Just Don't Understand*)—then toddlers and adults speak entirely different languages. So when your kids do something *really* outrageous—like running out on a busy street or yanking on the cord and knocking over the Mr. Coffee or smothering the new baby or punching the mailman in the groin—logic does not work. You can't explain right and wrong to two-year-olds. They just have to know in no uncertain terms that whatever it is, it's not okay.

Of course, yelling (or a good growling) works up to a point, especially if you can work up something really deep and stern. And so does banishment, though all of my grown kids later informed us that being sent to your room with all your toys and books is not really punishing. But nothing is as swift and sure and pointed as an open palm swatting a covered bottom.

The technique itself is very simple: take the toddler's upper arm in your left hand, turn her sideways, and then swat her with your open right palm on her bottom. Never anyplace else, never on bare flesh, and never hard enough to knock her out of your solid but nonsqueezing left-hand grasp. Sometimes it's good to follow it up with a "Don't ever do that again!" but I don't think it really matters. What matters is that they understand.

At some point, generally before kindergarten, spanking bottoms gives way to more reasoned forms of punishment. You can actually talk to them or yell at them and banish them at that point—and it means something. Or other.

Then the only form of corporal punishment allowable after toddlerhood is the *automobile swat*. It is an effective means of discipline when you are alone in the car with one or more screaming ninnies roughhousing in the backseat. I'm sure you've been there—either in the backseat of your own childhood or in the front seat more recently.

The technique again is quite simple. You begin with the peremptory growl or yell, then growl or yell louder, and then just when you think they will drive you out of your mind—and off the road—you put your left hand tightly on the wheel, hoist your right arm up and over the seat back, and while looking straight ahead at the road (very important), start swatting at anything you can hit.

Feel free to swat as hard as you can because the angle makes it almost impossible to have any real force behind it—and besides, after the first or second knee has been slapped, all the kids in the backseat have lifted their legs and are scrunched back toward the seat belts—way out of your reach.

Sometimes children laugh at parents doing the backseat swat because adults look ridiculous twisted around like that and because the slaps are so ineffectual. In those cases you have to do it again as soon as their legs are back down. And that will take care of that.

Finally, don't worry about turning your kids into ax murderers if you occasionally swat their bottoms. It seems to me that ax murderers come from truly abusive homes or homes where plain old everyday aggression is aggressively denied. Unlike many over-educated adults who have lost connection to the "isness" of the universe, children and little animals understand in their bones that aggression is a natural function of life—it cannot be obscured or denied, just appropriately directed. And with that knowledge they learn when aggressiveness is okay and when it is not.

Not a bad lesson for these violent times.

ARE YOU A WIMPY DAD?

Who wears the diapers in the family?

You Know You're a Wimp When . . .

- You have to ask your child's permission to go out Saturday night.

- Every other sentence in your phone conversation is to the little tot standing next to you.

- You're not sure if it's right to punish your child for painting the living room wall because you don't want to stifle his creativity.

- Your grocery cart is full of Twinkies, Cocoa Crispies, Cheese Doodles, Gummy Bears, Mountain Dew, and Hawaiian Punch.

- Your explanation of why it's not okay to hit Daddy is more than five words long. ("Don't ever do that again!")

- You ask your child to set the table and she says, "In a minute," and walks out of the room.

- Being alone with your kids makes you nervous.

- You clean your child's room while she's messing up the play-room, and vice-versa.

- Your child hides under his friend's bed when you arrive to pick him up . . . and the friend's mother is the only one who can get him out.

- Your three-year-old has the baby around the neck in a bear hug and you say, "He just loves her so much."

- You actually believe that the preschool teacher who says your child doesn't cooperate well in class is being insensitive to her needs.

THE ZEN OF
TOILET TRAINING

Floating away on a dream

> *Just as eating against one's will is injurious to health, so studying without a liking for it spoils the memory, and it retains nothing it takes in.*
>
> —LEONARDO DA VINCI

The evolution of potty training from child to child in most homes is a lot like the disappearing snapshot phenomenon.

You know how it goes: with the first child every moment of wakeful drooling and angelic sleep is recorded simultaneously by video and still cameras. With number two, however, the video cam is likely no longer functional and the album is predictably less ambitious and lacks the pithy commentary. And with number three (four, five, six . . .) the production of pictures grows proportionally smaller until at some point the album is replaced by a carton full of miscellaneous photographs of several unidentifiable infants, one or two of whom may be your own.

And so it is with potty training. With number one, the preparation begins long before the onset of the "new semester" in the tot's life. Books are read, pediatricians consulted, extensive equipment purchased, and a schedule devised to best meet the needs of parent and child without one impinging on the other's well-defined notions of self-determination and intestinal fortitude.

This is serious business; everyone in the early childhood game agrees that this is a most delicate and important developmental stage in a child's life, and one does not want to scar the little poop production machine forever with an inappropriate or insensitive approach to what is a natural and healthy human biological function.

With number two, however, the high anxiety has been dropped a notch or two. Basically you're too tired from having two kids to use up all that energy being detail oriented. Second round parents still schedule potty sessions, and still read four or five Berenstain Bears books per session, but not with the same enthusiasm and certainly not with the same degree of conviction.

By the advent of number three (and four and beyond), however, the total extent of parental involvement in potty training often consists of tossing a pair of training pants on the unmade bed and saying, "Your diaper days are over, Bucko. Get yourself dressed and ready for breakfast—and don't have any accidents."

And so it was for us (vis-à-vis pictures and toilet training). Cael, Patti, and I spent a month's worth of hours in the bathroom, reading books, sounding bright and cheery and supportive when there was nothing coming out, and cheering with great pride when something did. And, yes, there were several occasions when Cael was so proud of his production that we didn't flush for a long time so that we could all admire his good work. Along the way, we grew quite concerned when Roz and Dennis Read's overachieving son Evan was diaper-free (day and night!) while Cael still considered the world his toilet. But he eventually made it.

With Nancy we still had all the old equipment from Cael (the bathroom potty, the living room potty, the van potty, etc.) and even used it occasionally and cheered when she made it to the bathroom without an "accident," but we had lost our illusions that we were building her self-esteem; we just wanted to get her out of diapers because Addie was already born and filling them with abandon.

As for Addie, I think she pretty much toilet trained herself. I don't remember. Same thing with Clover. Anyway, they both figured it out somehow.

My revelation about the Zen of toilet training came with Danny. He was just past his third birthday and probably 90 percent trained, and whether or not he was psychologically and physiologically ready to gain 100 percent control of his excretory functions, we certainly were.

We were on our way home from Hatteras Island and had stopped for a picnic just before getting on the Chesapeake Bay Bridge Tunnel when little Danny had an accident. While it didn't seem to faze him a bit—he was running around, chasing his sisters and brothers, falling on his butt, and laughing some more—his siblings were totally grossed out.

"Change his diapers!" they yelled. "He stinks, pee-yew!"

"He doesn't wear diapers," I said calmly, as if that had anything to do with the stench that hovered in the humid air around our littlest boy.

"So, change his underpants! Just please clean him up!" Nancy, the neat and tidy daughter, was making gagging sounds, followed by Addie and Clover, who looked like they might puke. Thirteen-year-old Cael couldn't believe that he was stuck in a family like this.

And so I cleaned him up, but not happily. And not without some grave concern for the lateness of his development in this area. Driving over the bridge, I began to wax psychological, wondering if the periodic accidents were a form of passive aggression against his large busy family who didn't pay him enough attention; I worried that we hadn't scheduled enough potty sessions, that we hadn't read to him, that we didn't cheer loudly enough when he succeeded, that we flatly refused to save his gargantuan efforts afterward.

Midway across the twenty-three-mile span I grew panicky that they wouldn't allow him in nursery school in September, that he'd be frightfully humiliated on the playground and, spinning out beyond reason, much later on in high school. I broke out into a cold sweat with miragelike visions of a grown man wearing adult-size Pampers, rubber pants, and extra-large overalls with pockets full of diaper wipes.

I promised myself that I'd make an appointment with the pediatric psychologist as soon as we got home.

But as we approached the second tunnel on the span, the bridge disappearing out ahead and the massive Chesapeake Bay all around, I first panned the rearview mirror at Danny's four older siblings (and the miserable job we had done with their basic training) and then straight ahead at the endless line of cars full of children heading toward Virginia Beach—cars full of smart parents, stupid parents, hip parents, square parents, good parents, bad parents, black parents, yellow parents, white parents—and suddenly understood that probably 99 and 44/100 percent of their children get potty trained. What's the difference between twenty-six months and thirty-two months? Mostly, everyone gets potty trained in this life.

It was a real revelation.

As we drove across Fisherman's Island, I finally understood that Danny would be totally ready when he was totally ready. I caught his eye in the rearview mirror and blew him a kiss. He didn't understand, I'm sure, but he blew me one off his chubby little paws. And that was the last time he had an accident.

A COMMODE IS A COMMODE IS A COMMODE

A belated apology to Sears

> *Zen has no secrets other than thinking about birth and death.*
>
> —TAKEDA SHINGEN

As I've previously suggested, Patti and I have little to offer new potty trainers except the conviction that whatever well-meaning parents do to help their kids will eventually work. The problem, as the following story shows, is that no one knows precisely when it will work.

In the fall of 1971, shortly after Patti and I became home owners of a fifty-year-old beauty (a white Victorian with green trim on a double city lot on the east side of Milwaukee), we proudly went shopping one afternoon for a toilet seat, towel bar, bath mat, and shower curtain at Sears. Tagging along behind us was our little two-year-old terror, Cael. He was dressed rather nattily in his Wrangler elastic waist jeans, a Brewers T-shirt, a pair of blue-and-red Keds—and underneath it all were brand-new Winnie the Pooh training pants, which seemed to function as a training tool 50 percent of the time and as a sieve the other 50 percent.

So, somewhere between some absurdly intense discussions

over the worthiness of ceramic towel bars as opposed to plastic or metal and an argument over the value of double as opposed to single shower curtains, Cael wandered off and we temporarily lost sight of the little jock.

At first neither of us was terribly concerned when we didn't see him in the immediate vicinity—after all, it was 1971 and it was Milwaukee—but we did want to find him before he broke something or suddenly realized that we were no longer in his sight and began to howl like Elmer Fudd befuddled again by Daffy Duck. I called his name. Patti called his name.

There was no answer.

So while I checked bathwares, Patti roamed through appliances, and when we met up again in hardware and plumbing neither of us had found him. "Where is he?" I demanded, as if it were Patti's responsibility alone to be watching him every second. She had a terrified look that must have mirrored my own.

It was then that we turned and saw the young prince. I can't describe the relief that instantly washed over me, but it was very short-lived. There he was on his throne, only it wasn't quite a throne, it was a floor model of a light blue Kohler toilet. And his Wrangler jeans were no longer stretched tight around his fat belly, they were down around his red-and-blue Keds. And his cute little face was not that alabaster smoothness that we loved to catch in Kodacolor, it was bright red and scrunched up as if he was taking a crap.

And that, we realized a microsecond later, was exactly what he was doing.

Patti and I dropped the shower curtain and towel bars and raced down the aisle in a desperate attempt to try to stop him before anything unseemly occured, but the earthy aroma that greeted us as we approached our smiling urchin signaled our failure.

"Look! Look! Look!" he said hopping down off the throne. "I did it! I did it! I went potty!" I looked down into the shiny waterless bowl. Yes, he had. And with a vengeance, I might add.

Now, there was a real moral dilemma facing us. Our little potty matriculant had finally made it all the way to the bowl on his own after I can't tell you how many near misses. He had climbed to the top. He had grabbed the brass ring.

What were we going to do? Yell at him? Punish him for doing exactly what we'd been begging him to do for months? Besides, how could we ever explain the difference between a real potty and a floor model?

And another thing, what were we going to tell the store manager? What the hell could we tell the store manager?

We looked around. No one was there. We glanced at each other like high school sophomores who had just broken a window at school, silently mimed the universal *eek!* expression, and while Patti pulled up Cael's pants, I put the lid down on the toilet and the three of us racewalked out of the store across the parking lot and into the Dodge van.

It was a terribly immature thing to do, I'll admit. And I've often thought of the dozens of shoppers who imagined they smelled something rancid . . . and the hapless customer shopping for a light blue commode who lifted the lid on the floor model . . . and the horrified look on the salesman's weary face . . . but what else could we have done?

I don't know. I simply do not know. *Mea culpa. Mea culpa. Mea maxima culpa.* In that moment I achieved the heart and soul of a little child. If you could see me now, you'd see my arms open wide, palms up in the universal pose of cluelessness.

ZEN AND THE ART OF GETTING UNSTUCK

Getting a penis unstuck from a zipper

The foolish reject what they see, not what they think; the wise reject what they think, not what they see.

—HUANG PO

Pain is unavoidable in this life.

I'm not sure whether that is a Zen principle or an axiom of life that spans all theologies and cultures, but, as nearly all parents understand, there is no greater pain than the pain of a child. And no more soul-splitting sound than that of a toddler screeching in agony in the next room.

Children, especially small children, find themselves in excruciating pain perhaps twenty or thirty times a day. They stumble into the sides of tables, they stub their little toes, they bite their tongues, they burn their tongues, they cut themselves, they touch hot stoves, they skin their knees, they get splinters, and they get the double whammy of splinters gouged out by their needle-wielding mothers or fathers.

(Actually, I said fathers just to be fair and enlightened, but other than my friend Bruce Schenker I don't know any dads who do the home surgeries, even dad doctors. Perhaps it's because fathers pride themselves on being able to fix things for their families, and a child's pain is generally unfixable until it fixes itself. Perhaps it's got something to do with how women, by way of childbirth, truly understand that pain, like everything else in life, really does pass. Frankly, I don't know the answer. In my New Age Zen, however, not knowing is knowing.)

Anyway, with seven kids, I have been a party to the entire pantheon of minor childhood scrapes and bruises, from bleeding heads to fingers caught in car doors to broken bones and mind-altering concussions. But, trust me, there is no pain, no howling, no sense of fatherly powerlessness like a little guy with his little penis stuck in a zipper—and his mother out for the afternoon. Trust me.

Cael was five—Nancy a tubby ball of oneness—and the three of us were just hanging around the warm house on a cold fall Saturday afternoon while Patti was out for a few hours. I was in that Zen zone of fatherly unconsciousness—playing without playing, hearing without listening, speaking without talking, agreeing to everything without agreeing to anything.

Suddenly there was an otherworldly cry of agony from the other side of the house. I won't recount for you the horrors that I imagined as I raced through the kitchen of our old farmhouse, clomping through the dining room and bursting into the bathroom where the howling was growing in strength and intensity like an air-raid siren.

The look on my little guy's face as he stood paralyzed in front of the toilet was a study in Job-like pain. If it could have been translated, it would have said, "I didn't do anything bad. Why is this horrible thing happening to me?" And the yowling was almost unearthly.

As a member of the local rescue squad, I was somewhat accustomed to *acting* calm in the face of medical emergencies. But seeing my little boy with his little penis stuck in a zipper (a small piece of skin caught between the metal yanker and a tooth) I immediately lost my enlightened detachment: I spun around to yell for Patti (the needle wielder, the walking Heimlich maneuver,

Ms. Calm-in-a-medical-storm), and then spun back in the horrific realization that I was alone in the house—and I alone had to do something to stop the pain. And the yowling.

At first glance I thought that all I needed to do was what I figured Patti would do: simply give a brief but utterly painful yank on the zipper to set him free. And he would be free. But on closer inspection I saw that the piece of skin was caught firmly in the metal teeth. Who knows what would come off if I just yanked? I was not prepared to deal with the possibilities.

I momentarily considered calling the rescue squad, but the idea of the dispatcher's voice crackling on scanners all over town saying "Penis caught in zipper at One Coffey Lane" convinced me that the problem was best solved privately. Meanwhile, Cael was screeching, spinning around and around while I was pacing back and forth in the small bathroom, praying that somehow—miraculously—the penis had unstuck itself.

It hadn't. I picked him up. He screamed. I put him down. He screamed. The only thing I could think of was how the weight of the jeans on his stuck penis only increased the stinging pain. So I reached into the drawer and pulled out a pair of big sewing scissors. Cael took one look at the long shiny blades and the screaming turned to squealing.

He tried to run away, but with a penis stuck in a zipper, well, you know. I started cutting from the cuff of one leg and snipped up to the crotch along the seam of the zipper and through the thick waistband. A few more snips and then down the back side and one leg was removed.

By the time I was finished cutting, Cael was standing there bare bottomed with a three-inch square of jean and zipper hanging off his raw penis.

And he was still screeching.

Now what? I thought of pliers. I thought of Vaseline. I thought of Wesson oil. I meditated on the unique properties of penises the world over. I thought about how penises have lives of their own. I thought of my own penis. I scooped him up and strode over to the bathtub, turned on the cold tap, and waited until there was half a foot of frigid water and laid him down in the cold tub. He squirmed. He yanked on my hair. He pleaded to get out. He yowled as if I were torturing him.

And two seconds later the patch of zipper was floating on the surface of the suddenly still water. And the look on his face was of pure cosmic relief.

The blissful ahhhhhhhhhness of getting unstuck.

UNTANGLING THE KNOTTED STRANDS OF LIFE

The Zen of getting bubble gum out of hair

Action should culminate in wisdom.
—BHAGAVAD GITA

Patti was down in Florida visiting her father. There was nothing remarkable about the trip or the fact that I was alone with the brood for several days, but I was admittedly a little concerned about four-year-old Elizabeth. She was still so cosmically attached to Patti that mere separation had the potential to tip the homeostatic balance.

(The previous time Patti went away, Elizabeth's cold escalated into a 104-degree fever and we sat up all night shooting hallucinogenic monsters out of her delirium.)

I was spending a typical spring Saturday going to the dump and taxiing kids all over town, ending up down in Wallkill with Bay and Elizabeth to watch Danny play soccer. And I was prepared, as a father of seven should be prepared, with a blanket, a few well-chosen politically correct toys, some wholesome snacks, ten percent 100-percent-pure fruit juices, sun block, and a trusty bag of candy and gum if things got testy.

I won't go into the particulars of how we got to the candy

and gum stage so early in the second half of the game—any parent can easily conjure up an applicable situation—but we were there nevertheless. Bay, who had grown bored watching packs of twelve-year-old boys fruitlessly chasing a round ball, was playing in a dirt pile with some other dirty kids, and Elizabeth was happily chewing on some (sugar-free) bubble gum at my side. And, as such, I was enjoying my first few unfettered moments of the game, which was suddenly the most interesting and important event in my life.

I actually began to care if *we* won(!), and thus lost conscious awareness of the portable voice machine at my side. She was babbling on as if we were actually having a conversation, and I was nodding and adding an occasional clueless *hmmmmmm*, and the game (and the day) was heating up, and I was growing increasingly annoyed at the crowd of enemy parents nearby who kept cheering every time one of the Wallkill kids made a good play.

So it was a good five minutes before I looked down to see why Elizabeth had suddenly grown quiet. But five minutes was enough for her to have taken the wad of well-chewed pink gum and stretched it in both directions across her face, around and around her neck and up into her hair and down the other side. Up, down, across, and sideways—and then back again. All over her face. In her ear. The skin on her neck wrinkled and pressed together. Her long hair a tangled mass of deranged clumps.

All I could think of in the horror of the moment was Patti stepping off the plane in two days and seeing her baby girl with a crew cut. (I'm not sure if it was my mother or someone else's mother, but I do have a motherly voice hidden deep in the audiotape files of my memory saying, "We're going to have to cut that gum out of your hair!")

However, from years of experience with bubble gum stuck to noses and lips, I did know that if you rubbed the chewed gum on the pieces stuck on the skin, the stuck parts should come off.

So I snatched what was left of the wad out of her mouth and started rubbing her face and neck (and arms and legs). Owing to some principle of anatomy that I don't understand, the gum came easily off her nose and lips and limbs, and easily enough off her red ears, but the neck was a totally different story. The stuck gum just grew dirtier and dirtier as I rubbed and scoured and stretched the tender skin. And when Elizabeth began to whimper and plead for me to stop—and the Wallkill parents glared at me as if I were a child abuser—I turned to her hair, trying in vain to separate the tangled sticky strands until she let out a shriek that sounded like the town fire whistle.

At the end of the game (we lost), I gathered up Bay, who was covered with a sweaty paste of dirt, Danny, who was one massive grass stain after spending the entire game perfecting his slide tackle, and whimpering Elizabeth, and headed silently to the car and home, the bath, and the scissors.

Driving has always been a transcendent experience for me, a chance to zone out and go on automatic pilot while I consider the vagaries of existence. It's a Zen state that many fathers attain, they just don't know it's Zen. And the drive up Route 208 that afternoon was no different. Somewhere between Ireland Corners and Dressel's orchards I recalled someone someplace saying something about peanut butter and gum in hair. I think it was Donna Ciliberto who heard about it from Linda Ackert.

I had nothing to lose. As soon as we got home, I snatched the Skippy out of the pantry, reached three fingers into the wide mouth, and grabbed a fistful of the creamy stuff. Elizabeth looked equally horrified and amused as I spread the gooey stuff on her neck and then all through her hair, massaging it into her scalp as if it were shampoo.

She giggled like we were kids doing something really bad behind Mom's back. And I laughed as I squished my fingers through her hair because she wasn't crying, because it felt like we were doing something bad behind Mom's back, and because the tangles were actually coming unstuck! It was magic!

When Patti came home two days later, Elizabeth and I picked her up at the airport with clean, brushed hair, smirks on our faces, and the knowledge that action does indeed culminate in wisdom. And thus my advice: while I can't in good conscience endorse a specific product relative to the untangling of one's "stuckness," any brand probably works as well as any other, but I'd stay away from chunky or the kinds that mix jelly in the jar.

BUDDHIST (AFTERNOON) DELIGHT

Sex, lies, and Cocoa Crispies

> *If we achieve satori and the satori shows, like a bit of dogshit stuck on the tip of our nose, that is not so good.*
> —TAISEN DESHIMARU

Another axiom of parental life: when children get wind of sexual electricity buzzing between Mom and Dad—and it definitely is in the wind—they will do everything in their power to cut the lines and sabotage the glorious event.

It's not that the little imps want to rob parents of whatever small pleasures adults find in life—although I don't really think that parental pleasure is on any healthy child's agenda—but I do believe that all children understand intuitively the perilous ramifications of sex between parents. That's why babies always seem to wake up or toddlers barge into your room just when things are really heating up. They know in their fragile little bones that sex equals baby and baby spells danger, not only for the infant who must protect her or his milk supply but also for older children who comprehend the economics of food and time and the profound impact of one more sister or brother on family dynamics.

So, it's in their best interests to keep you celibate.

But life, of course, has its own devious pleasures. Just about the time that coitus interruptus seems like the only coitus there is in young parents' lives, the joys of "napping" in the afternoons opens up to them like lotus blossoms. And, indeed, there is nothing quite so lovely and spiritually elevating as a Saturday or Sunday "nap," you and your sweetheart alone and unfettered for an hour or more of afternoon delight.

Naps are wonderful oases for young parents because, in general, toddlers not only need and want their daily siestas, they don't resist them with the same steely ferocity as going "nigh-nigh." Even infants know from their limited experience that a nap is only a temporary respite from the joys of driving parents crazy, and that when they wake up there's still a whole day of pooping left to achieve purpose in life.

When Cael was a toddler it was easy to achieve that kind of satori in the afternoon. If the opportunity and desire arose, we would simply slip in the sack as soon as he curled up with his "banky" in the crib. Sometimes we even slept, another kind of satori for the diaper weary.

The problem with achieving afternoon delight comes with the addition of one or more children into the household. Unless they all nap—and nap at the same time—those private little thirst-quenching oases from the rigors of parenting threaten to become little more than memories or mirages or mmmmm-rated fantasies disappearing in thin air.

And that's when you have to be opportunistic, sneaky, dishonest, and utterly libido-driven. Like a teenager. Which is what you are in your heart anyway. Which is when the quest for the next level of satori truly begins.

As men and women all over the planet know from their own devious teenage years, there is nothing steamier, sexier, or quite so frustratingly exciting as making out on the couch after your parents have gone to sleep—or gone out for the evening. But, as we also know, such pleasures involve planning and higher-level consciousness of the metarealities of hidden sexual conduct. Parents must also think ahead.

The technique for achieving Stage Two afternoon satori is not very complex, but does involve strict adherence to four simple rules:

RULE I : Be certain that your partner is on the same page of the same Anne Rice book as you are. There is no greater sense of worldly disappointment than setting up a romantic tryst and making a swan dive into the marriage bed only to find that she really does want to take a nap.

RULE 2: No one except the conspirators should ever get wind of your plans. No public displays of affection. All kissing, petting, rubbing against, grabbing, snorting (and all other animal noises) must be held in check. You must be utterly parental in your demeanor. And foreplay must be accomplished in total privacy: in the next room, in the bathroom, behind the kitchen counter, anywhere but in front of your children. Remember, it's in the air. Be careful.

RULE 3: Don't get creative. The tried-and-true nap scam is the only reasonable path to follow. Children will snicker right in your face if you say something like "Mom and I will be doing some important work in the bedroom, so don't disturb us." They don't have a great deal of respect for work, especially since the two of you complain about it in front of them all the time. And they certainly won't allow you to slip away unnoticed for as long as it takes to accomplish your mutual goals. All children have a built-in sonar detector that drives them to seek out and find lost parents every ten to fifteen minutes.

However, kids understand that a sleeping parent is almost always better than an alert one. They want Mom or Dad around in case something bad happens, but they also know that a sleeping parent will never know if they do fun bad things like sneak into the cookies or play in the sink. Plus, they know you'll be up soon, so their own sense of illicitness will give them almost as much pleasure as your own sense of illicitness will give you. It's perfect.

RULE 4: Cocoa Crispies. There's no reasonable excuse for keeping sugary cereals in the house, except for moments like these; and then they become an integral phase of the final plans. Before leaving the room, you snap on your fatherly voice and recite everything that they must not—ever—touch or do, and then say, "I'm going to pour you a cup of Cocoa Crispies in case you get hungry." Of course they take the bribe. That way they not only get rid of you but get paid for it. And it keeps them busy for at least a little while.

And that's it. You disappear behind the locked door and experience the pleasures of the here and now while your children are discovering new and devious ways to entertain themselves.

One last caveat: neither you nor your partner (nor the bed or the floorboards) must make a sound while you're in the throes of impassioned pleasures—and you must not say anything or look too blissful after it's all over. If they even think you're doing something so outlandish under their noses, you'll look like you have dogshit on your noses and you'll never again know the secret pleasures of afternoon satori.

5

Early Satori:
The Peaceful Era Before
the Teenage Wars

THE ZEN BROWNIE LEADER

*How a father leads a troop of little girls
into the wilderness when there is
no mother in sight*

> *Zen teaches nothing; it merely enables us to wake up and
> become aware. It does not teach, it points.*
>
> —D. T. SUZUKI

I am one of the few men in North America—perhaps the world—
who can recite the Brownie pledge, sing "I've got something in
my pocket that belongs across my face . . ." (complete with correct hand movements), order and bestow badges, teach the prin-
ciples of Juliette Low, as well as choreograph and direct a solemn
but Kodak-cute moving up ceremony that includes a scripted
and abridged three-minute version of "The Brownie Story." And
I know which snacks refresh but do not stain.

Patti became the Brownie leader of Troop 242 in 1979, when
Nancy was a first grader. And if I may say so, she was—and remains—the quintessential Brownie leader, as comfortable with pa-
pier mâché as tying knots and digging latrines. During those early
years I was the dutiful dad and husband, attending all ceremonies
with camera in hand, setting up the yard for the campouts, and
maintaining consciousness during Nancy's stirring monologues
about badge acquisition and campfire safety. But I was not, I admit, a Brownie aficionado. I just went along to get along.

For some reason, though—I can't remember which pregnancy got in the way—she had to step aside for a year and the
troop was left leaderless.

So, without much prodding and even less comprehension of
the duties that go along with the job, I undertook the hallowed
position of leader. Actually, Patti deftly positioned me so that I
thought I actually wanted the job: she mentioned offhandedly
one day that another local father, Dick Geuss, had been a Brownie
leader for several years. Then, several minutes later, she wondered aloud why more men didn't have the "stuff" to lead a troop
of first-, second-, and third-grade girls.

My manhood and my fatherhood thus challenged, I immediately enrolled in a Brownie leader workshop with a dozen women
of all shapes, sizes, and social fortunes. As I walked into that first
meeting, every woman in the room glared at me with a curious
mixture of cautious wonder and extreme distrust. Behind the
smile and the limp handshake of each mother was the (neon)
flashing sign: OH LORD, ANOTHER DICK GEUSS, ONLY THIS ONE HAS
LONG HAIR. And behind that: *What the hell is he doing here? My
husband wouldn't be caught dead in this place!*

But I persevered the way that men always persevere with
women when we're out of our manly element: we act inept. By the
second meeting practically every woman in the group was vying
for the chance to help me make a "dream catcher." If I didn't win
their respect, I did win their approval—and their certification.

From there on, I organized Brownie meetings, I sang the
Brownie songs, I pledged the Brownie pledge, I served the
Brownie snacks, I did Brownie crafts that I didn't think men
were capable of doing, and in the spring I went to a council
meeting and announced my intentions to take the girls into the
woods to learn to identify animal tracks.

My announcement, which I anticipated would be met with
great enthusiasm, was followed by a most uncomfortable silence
and a jittery leap to the next item on the agenda. A few days
later the processed word came down from "council" that I was

not allowed to take the girls for a hike without chaperons. A single adult male was not sanctioned to be alone in the woods ("To the woods! No, not the woods.") with innocent little Brownies.

I guess they figured that in the basement of the Reformed Church I would be able to keep my dark side in check, but out in the mountain wilderness of New Paltz I might forget all civilized restraint and . . . what? *(He does have all those kids!)*

Deeply offended—and full of the self-righteousness of false accusation—I prepared to take on the council. I'd write letters. I'd threaten to go to court. I'd go to court. I'd take it all the way to Washington. This was defamation of character, institutional bias, reverse discrimination of the worst sort! And, besides, what the hell was I going to do with the little buggers now that it was warm outside?

Patti, who fully intended to return to scouting the next year—and who understood the parochial machinations of Girl Scout leadership—advised me against making a federal case out of it. "Just do it," she said. "No one up there will ever find out."

(I feel I should mention that she said "Just do it!" a decade and a half before the cynics at Nike made it sound like we were hearing it for the first time.)

And so I did it. We wandered the woods and swamps and saw deer tracks, bunny tracks, raccoon, and maybe (just maybe) bear tracks, and by the end of the day no one could remember or recognize what they saw, except the deer droppings, which looked a lot like bunny pellets. But it was fun (even if I had to carry Olivia Harrison practically the whole way because she didn't want to get mud on her white shoes) and I learned a real lesson about the way children learn. You invite them along into the wilderness and they learn things they never knew before. You just do it. Everyone finds something to take home with them. Even if it's poison ivy.

THE ZEN SOCCER COACH

And the demonic inner child in a lawn chair

You don't need Little League. You don't even need nine kids. Four is plenty—a pitcher, a batter, and a couple of shaggers. You can play ball all day long. My kids used to try to get me out there, but I'd just say 'Go play with your brothers.' If kids want to do something, they'll do it. They don't need adults to do it for them.

—YOGI BERRA

When Cael was old enough to play for the local Little League team, I had to decide between joining the elite coaching ranks of gruff-throated fathers with whistles around their necks or the lawnchair brigade of baby boomer dads. It was a nonchoice.

As a former three-sport "star" at Wheatley High (blazing more brightly with each passing year), long-suffering Dodger fan, and perennial boy inhabiting the shell of an aging man's body, I knew all too well about fathers and sons and whose cogliones are really on the line when a little boy steps up to the plate. (At the time, I was still quite naive and did not know that sports moms also have *cogliones*.)

So I chickened out. I was afraid that I didn't know enough about skills development, game strategy, and fostering the necessary toughness to serve parents whose sons were destined to be the future Pete Roses of the western world. It would be humbling for me—and abject humiliation for Cael—if I stood in front of a pack of bulldog-faced sires and tried to explain my philosophy that sports are supposed to be fun.

However, when Nancy was nine and the newly enlightened coed town soccer league was searching (i.e., begging) for coaches to lead their teams, I strapped on the whistle and the jock strap and headed into the fray. At the time most people didn't know squat about soccer, so I figured the parents wouldn't know if I was doing a good job or not. Besides, as the father of a daughter I'd be cut a lot more slack for my wimpy managerial style.

Actually, the first few weeks of practices as the head of the Blue Raiders were murder. I don't know what happened, but in the time it took for me to receive my whistle and stick it in my mouth, I was transformed from a happy hippie coach (*winning isn't everything*) to the reincarnation of Vince Lombardi (*winning is the only damn thing*).

I spent hours planning for the ninety-minute practice sessions, devising fun but educational ball handling exercises, interspersing pep talks with skill development modules, interjecting strategy discussions into scrimmages punctuated with well-chosen insights about the meaning of sport and life. I told them that while there was nothing wrong with losing, we really *had* to win.

Honestly, it was awful. I spent most of the practices trying to make them all listen to my pearls of soccerly wisdom—and they wwouldn't listen. I felt like a substitute teacher forcing the kids to do homework after working all day long at school. I was miserable. And the kids, who only wanted to run around and yell and play soccer in the crisp fall air, were miserable.

Then came our first game. Shortly after the opening whistle it became apparent that they didn't remember anything I had told them about positions and passing. They didn't even remember how to do a proper throw-in. And apparently the opposing team didn't remember a thing their coach told them. On the green field were two packs of chimpanzees, distinguishable only by the color of their shirts, chasing a ball that kept skidding away from them. It looked like a lot of fun.

And it might have been fun, except for the parents behind us. Hordes of them in lawn chairs lining the field, cheering one child's domination over another, berating the poor volunteer refs, screaming venomously when a sixty-pounder side-stepped a hundred-pound charging bull, and groaning in undisguised disgust when an easy goal kick was missed or when a child reasonably shied away from a three-mile-high header.

In the second half, an exasperated father stormed over to me and started drawing attack strategies in the dirt with a stick. I thanked him and said I was just happy at this point if they were all going in the right direction. He looked over at another red-faced father and shook his sorry head as if I were not only beneath contempt but beyond any hope for salvation.

At that moment I decided to stop being a coach and allowed the kids the same pleasure of playing soccer I had when I was a kid and there were no adults in sight. And we did okay, winning nearly as many games as we lost, celebrating the end of the season at JD's soft ice-cream stand.

Two years later with Addie's team, I coached less, encouraged more, and gradually learned to enjoy the dance of life from the sidelines. Thanks in no part to my coaching style, we went undefeated. With Clover's team, which might have gone winless except for a couple of really lucky breaks, I began to achieve a state of coachless coaching.

So by the time Danny came along, I would spend one practice session working on various kicks and the rules of the game—and then set them free for the rest of the season. During scrimmages I occasionally mentioned moving the ball in the right direction (a major victory with at least two of the kids), playing your position (as opposed to everyone on both teams swarming around the ball), and the benefits of passing (forget it). We won as many as we lost. Not bad at all.

If the league ever allows me to coach again, I think my managerial strategy will be simply to give the kids a ball and allow them to play soccer. They'll figure it out. I'll sit on the sidelines with a cup of coffee and a newspaper just in case someone gets hurt or needs to go to the bathroom.

And before the first game, I will schedule a mandatory parents' contest where the kids will sit in lawn chairs on the sidelines and yell like obnoxious children when the players fail to charge an opponent or shy away from a tall header or miss an easy kick—or get tired and rest for a minute.

As Yogi says, the kids figure it out by themselves.

JUST SAY YES

When yes is no and no is yes

> *There is no way you can use the word "reality" without quotation marks around it.*
>
> —JOSEPH CAMPBELL

Nearly ten years ago I was sitting on the back deck, half sleeping, half listening to a group of kids on the swing set. One yelled, "Let's pretend that yes is no and no is yes!" The rest, dangling and sliding and spinning wildly, screamed with such glee at her suggestion that I was struck dumb—i.e., awakened—by the simple beauty of the vision.

The message was so elegant: yes is no and no is yes. All kids in all times have done the same thing, turning the world inside out to see the world as it truly is. Moments later they raced up to the deck and stood in front of me, smiling, dirty-faced, and panting.

"Hi. Are you all having fun?"

"No." A few giggled.

"Would you like a drink?"

They looked at each other and giggled some more. "No."

"Would you like some cookies?"

"No!" they roared in unison.

"Would you . . . like to wash the dishes?"

"Yes!!"

"Mop the floor?"

"Yes!!!"

One more question about cleaning the toilets and they were rolling on the rug, squealing hysterically.

The encounter soon fizzled, however, because the kids were sophisticated enough to know when to take the cookies and scram. They left and I went back to the window to digest an emerging epiphany about the nature of reality. Indeed, yes is no and no is yes.

But it was not until Elizabeth actually demonstrated the principle many years later that I truly understood its application in real life.

It was probably Patti who discovered the little puddles of water around the algae-encrusted fish tank. In truth, it doesn't matter. After determining that there was no leak from the tank, she wiped up the water, checked the fish in the murky tank, and found one missing. Just one.

She quickly convened a family meeting where we all stood around the bubbling tank like men stand around the open hood of a disabled car trying to bluff their way through a problem they simply do not understand.

The older sleuths (Clover, Danny, Patti, and I) soon pointed our collective fingers directly at Sammy the cat. All the evidence suggested Sammy, a real scoundrel if there ever was one, was the killer. He slunk away as if he still had the taste of tropical fish in his mouth.

Bay, who likes to believe the best of everyone, including cats like Sammy, wondered if the fish could have just jumped out of the tank all by itself. Danny made a face. "If the fish jumped out of the tank, Sherlock, where is it now?"

That's when we first heard Elizabeth's little voice behind us: "The fish is not in my pocketbook."

"What?"

"The fish is *not* in my pocketbook."

Ahhhhhhhh. Patti raced over to the playroom and found Elizabeth's pocketbook and the little fish, which was miraculously still alive, and quickly returned him to his home in the murky depths.

And with heart full of joy I ran to the mirror and read my lips: "No, yes is no. And yes, no is yes."

No? Yes.

THE RULES OF
THE ROAD

*Telling Danny the truth about
the way adults tell the truth*

Do as I say, not as I do.
—EVERY PARENT

Nine-year-old Danny and I were zipping along on the New York State Thruway, radio blaring, not saying a word to each other. Out of nowhere, it seemed, he leaned over and checked the speedometer and then made the simple but pointed observation that everyone was speeding. It was true. I was going my normal "law abiding" sixty-three miles per hour and we were in the slow lane. Practically everyone was passing us.

In the face of the abject truth, it seemed pointless to make up excuses ("They don't really mean fifty-five") or outright lies ("Speedometers are often ten miles per hour incorrect") or, worst of all, offer him the "Do as we say, not as we do" speech. I turned down the radio and flatly agreed that most people don't follow rules exactly as they are laid out. I then tried being a good father and slowed down to fifty-four miles per hour, which felt more like twenty-four, and judging by the swerving cars I saw in my rearview mirror, almost caused several pileups.

When we arrived home, it took an extended visit to my "office" (you know, Dad's office with a sink and toilet and lots of magazines) to figure out what to say or do to explain the adult world's hypocrisies to a savvy nine-year-old—and still have him follow the rules.

As a member of the "Question Authority" generation, I guess I haven't been much of a rule follower myself, although I have made the usual accomodations along the way: I go to work, pay taxes, mow the lawn, honor my marriage, yadda, yadda, yadda. By and large I live between the lines. You know.

On the other hand—and solely for the purpose of making a point here—I'll admit that, among a host of other petty crimes and hypocrisies, I roll through stop signs and toss apple cores out the window into the woods, indiscretions that apparently have not eluded my errant boy.

In fact, being a smart kid, not much of the world's double standards have passed him by. At nine, he had already observed the big belly on the coach; he had complained that some of his teachers didn't do *their* homework; he knew from watching TV about corrupt politicians, child-molesting priests, drug-abusing athletes, depraved movie stars.

As such, I knew how difficult it would be to impress upon a fourth grader the importance of following rules when it is apparent that the rule makers break them as easily as little kids chomp into jawbreakers without a single fracture. I figured the truth was my only out.

So the next day Danny and I returned to the thruway to find out the truth about speeding in America. It was my job to keep the car at a steady sixty miles per hour, and it was Danny's job to count the number of cars that we passed as well as those that passed us.

He began counting as a carload of old ladies from New Jersey streaked by like a pace car leading a culturally diverse parade of two-, four-, and sixteen-wheeled vehicles that left us in the dust. At the Harriman toll plaza, thirty-two miles from our upstate exit, I figured the point was made.

Danny added up the numbers. It was a romp, a KO, a humiliating blow for the forces of law and order: 122 to nothing. Zip. I didn't pass a single vehicle on the entire stretch of highway. I didn't even brake.

We looked at each other and—what else was there to do?—laughed like little kids. And on the way home, each of us lost in the backroads of life's contradictions, Danny observed—all by his nine-year-old self—that most of the cars had not been zooming past us, and none were careening out of control. We figured that most of them were going sixty-five to seventy miles per hour. Then he wondered out loud what would happen if the speed limit was raised to sixty-five and soon thereafter answered his own question: everyone would go seventy-five to eighty.

We agreed that the world is a funny place. It isn't what it's supposed to be, but it actually resembles itself quite a lot. We returned home that day, my arm around his slender shoulders, going a steady fifty-nine, an acceptable compromise for two guys who had learned a lesson in real-world limits.

WHO WEARS THE BELT
IN YOUR FAMILY?

*Achieving complete misunderstanding
with one's child*

> *If the doors of perception were cleansed every thing to man
> would appear as it is, infinite.*
>
> —WILLIAM BLAKE

Sitting cross-legged on the unmade king-size bed, Bay looks
much smaller than his five years. He is watching me very intently, round chin resting in the smooth cup of his soft hand. I
am putting on my dark pinstriped suit, absorbed in ponderous
thought, barely aware of the youthful brown eyes that observe
my every move.

This is a significant event for both of us, if only for how seldom
it occurs. I rarely—rarely—wear a suit. As a teacher for more than
twenty years, I have "passed" with that tweedy patches-on-the-
elbows look. As a writer, I have gotten by with considerably less.

In fact, I have only owned one suit since I got married in
1968. Around the house it's jokingly called my wedding and funeral suit. Unfortunately, this morning I am not getting dressed
for a wedding. Staring through the oak-framed mirror into my
own deep-set eyes, I am searching for a clue to a question that
does not form in my mind or lips.

I have been to several funerals lately. I suppose that happens when you reach your midforties. The world seems considerably smaller to me now than it used to when I imagined everything was possible.

As I button the sleeves on my crisp white shirt, I am uncomfortably reminded of the dressing of the corpse in the beginning of the movie *The Big Chill*. A shiver runs like a frightened rabbit across my shoulder blades as I imagine myself a cold and helpless participant in my own final dressing for the world. "Joy to the World" is playing discordantly on the soundtrack.

In the mirror I see Bay tilt his head as I start to hum the tune "Jeremiah was a bullfrog . . ." and for a moment his soft quizzical countenance makes me sadder than I already am. A man's time with his children—his babies—is so short. It's never enough. Even with seven children spanning a whole generation, the years are not long enough, the days racing by like windows in speeding trains, their soft baby faces growing more angular and wary with each passing hour. I was not much more than a boy when Cael was born. I will be sixty when Elizabeth Bayou-Grace graduates from high school.

Stepping into the dark pressed trousers, I promise myself with great solemnity to spend more time with my family while I still have a chance. There is no better proof than this funeral for the father of one of Cael's friends that no one knows when his or her time will come. I make a covenant with my reflection to be fully alive in every passing moment of my days, not buried in my work or drugged by the TV. Life is no joke; not even a second is to be squandered frivolously.

As I pull up the zipper, press the button through the hole, and begin to thread the black belt through the loops, Bay slips off the big bed. By the time I yank the shiny buckle tight against my growling stomach, he is standing right next to me, his little face a few inches below my hip. As I reach for a tie, I see his mouth forming a thought.

"Dad?"

"Yes, Bay?"

"Dad, when I grow up," he says cranking his head to the side, "I want to be just like you."

The tears that wash over my eyes come on so suddenly that I must kneel, reaching for the slight shoulders and little head covered with soft brown hair. I ache to press him so close to me that we will never be apart, but he leans back as if there is still more to say, something that will illuminate the rest of my days: "Yup," nodding just like his older brothers, "when I grow up, Dad, I want to wear a belt every day!"

It was a perfect send-off to a funeral, though I'm not sure how successful I was in swallowing the smirk that kept sneaking through my lips like a cheap one-liner. When I got home and Bay jumped up into my arms, I hugged him for the one I missed earlier and also for the wonderful and terrible good sense that he brings to my life.

Then I threw off the suit and we sat around, wasting time.

IT'S NINE O'CLOCK: DO YOU KNOW WHERE YOUR CHILDREN ARE?

Forgetting Clover at the Vermilyes

> *When the mind is nowhere it is everywhere. When it occupies one tenth, it is absent in the other nine tenths.*
> —TAKUAN

Patti met Kitty Vermilye more than twenty years ago when she answered an ad in the local weekly for mothers interested in starting a play group. As Nancy and Lydia played together that first morning, the two mothers found a companionship of spirit that soon evolved to dragging their workaholic husbands to weekend get-togethers that their also socially resistant husbands tried desperately to avoid. And so, just as most married men would never have friends without their companionable wives, Steve and I became lifelong friends despite the fact that we've always been too busy to do anything together, except perhaps eat.

I don't recall exactly when the tradition began, but at some point in the late seventies, the Lewises and the Vermilyes started to eat Sunday dinners with each other, alternating houses by the week. Lopsided as it was (they have only two kids), Sunday evenings with Steve, Kitty, Lydia, and Jamie soon became a valued respite from the traffic of our increasingly busy and complicated lives.

One Sunday evening in 1984, like so many other Sunday evenings after a dinner full of the usual good laughter and spilled drinks and bad jokes, I nudged Patti and reminded her—as I often did in those days—that I had hours of papers to review before going to bed. It was Sunday night, but I was already completely absorbed within the crisscrossing realities of a Monday to be spent teaching at two different schools. We gathered the Lewis herd together, thanked our hosts once again for their graciousness, and piled into the mustard colored Vanagon.

In the time it took to insert *Highway 61 Revisited* into the tape player, my mind was in complete gridlock. I drove the cold van up the dirt road, bumping across the tracks onto Glen Circle, made a left on Forest Glen, another left on Route 208, and was a mile or two past Dressel's orchards when I suddenly experienced an odd sensation of lightness. The van actually felt less stable on the road. The energy felt incomplete. The center of gravity had shifted. Something was missing.

With headlights behind us illuminating the dark shapes in the seats I counted heads: one, two, three, four . . . four . . . four . . . FOUR! I flipped on the overhead lights and saw Cael, Nancy, Addie, and Danny squinting and scowling at the bright ceiling.

"Poochie," I called back over my shoulder, assuming she had fallen asleep. "Poochie? . . . Poochie!"

"Where's Clover?" Patti demanded of the kids, as if they, not us, were responsible for her. Cael, who never quite acknowledged that we had any real children after him, shrugged as if it were an irrelevant question. Nancy, who probably knew where Clover was but enjoyed the parental hysteria, merely looked out the window. And Addie, who was angry at Nancy and didn't hear the question, was still scowling at the light. Just then little Danny spoke up as nonchalantly as if he were talking about the weather, "Oh, she's upstairs playing with Jamie."

I jammed on the brakes, squealed through a jerky U-turn, and roared back up 208, a sickening lump forming in my stomach as we red-lined it back to Bridge Creek Road. Bumping down the dirt lane, Patti and I imagined our delicate little Clover curled up in a corner, crying hysterically, inconsolable, scarred for life, and doomed to an eternity on a psychoanalytic couch—or worse, dribbling and drooling in some asylum run by a man who looked and sounded like Mel Brooks. We skidded to a halt in front of the house and barged en masse through the door like the Six Stooges.

And there was little Clover, standing in the middle of her foster family with a toothless grin and a scowl and an embarrassed fistful of anger that would last for a day or maybe a week. Not a lifetime.

As the person in our family who has always proceeded through life with the fewest claims on the universe, her toothless grin told me a lot that night about the relationship between nowhere and everywhere. She forgave Patti and me our inexcusable lapse of concentration because, even at seven years old, she saw the nine tenths of life that we too often fail to see, and knew that precisely when she was nowhere in our thoughts, she was everywhere. Even before the best-selling book came along, Clover understood the meaning of the "unbearable lightness of being."

6

Nanto (or Hard-to-Penetrate Koan) and Teenage Boys

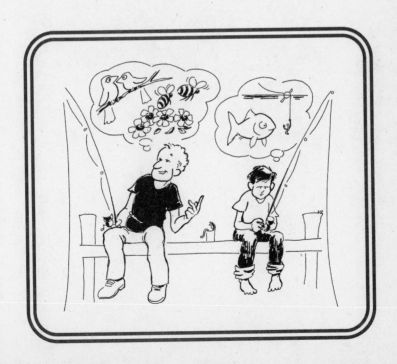

THE ZEN SEX TALK

The fine line between sex and sport

A young man is so strong, so mad, so certain, and so lost.
He has everything and is able to use nothing.
—THOMAS WOLFE

My own parent-child sex talk in 1959 was brief and to the point:
I was sitting on the green Naugahyde couch in the den of the
house on Candy Lane (yes again, Candy Lane) and watching the
television, when a dark figure passed across the door and an object of awkward dimensions came hurtling through the air and
landed to my right. Just as I recognized it as a book, a raspy
voice of unearthly quality mumbled, "Read this."

I won't swear to it, but after all these years I think the figure
was my mother, and seconds later I heard the same voice trail-
ing off down the hall saying something like, "If you have any
questions, just ask. . . ."

I picked up the book, thumbed my way to Chapter One, and
closed it as soon as I hit the words *fallopian tubes.* That was it.

Of course, I already knew just about everything there was to
know about women and sex from the local brain trust: Marshall
Diamond, Steven Weil, and the older wise presence down the
street, Bobby Jayson. (This was the same erudite crew that, a

few years earlier, had ridiculed and beat up Joe Rappaport for the totally outrageous and revolting claim—during a punchball game—that babies were made by the man putting his penis in the woman's vagina.)

Thus, I swore that when my kids came of age I would have open and honest and unembarrassing discussions with them about the joys and responsibilities of human sexuality.

My first opportunity to step up to bat, so to speak, was just before Cael's thirteenth birthday in July of 1982. My well-orchestrated plan was for us to go out to the woods and pitch a tent and fish and grill raw meat over an open fire and talk like real men. And I'd tell it all flat out. There did not exist a sexual subject I wouldn't cover from A(nuses) to Z(ippers).

We arrived, set up the tent, took a swim, tossed a baseball, did a little fishing, hiked around the pond, made a fire, cooked some dogs ... and all afternoon I kept waiting for the right ("organic") opportunity to introduce the subject. But of course the right opportunity never quite presented itself. Fathers and teenage sons don't normally find themselves talking about sex.

Several times during the day I asked if he had *any* questions "about anything at all," now that we were out in the woods and away from Mom and Nancy and Addie and Clover and Danny. But he had no clue as to what I was talking about. "No," he said, shaking his shaggy head, "I can't think of anything."

I knew in my heart, though, that once we got going on our talk, he'd have a million and one questions for me, and I'd answer every one as openly as I could—and when I couldn't, we'd laugh so hard we'd roll on the ground gasping for breath.

I just needed the right opening.

Hours passed in front of the fire; we talked about everything and nothing—mostly nothing, which is the way boys and their fathers seem to communicate best, faces forward, the road slipping endlessly behind—and still we hadn't touched on the nitty or the gritty.

So, right after some serious words about Thurman Munson's

RBI count, I jammed on the conversational brakes, popped the clutch, and made a hard right down Sex Lane: "Now that you're thirteen, Cael ... you must have some questions...." The groan that escaped his throat went down nine generations.

He locked his eyes over my left shoulder and shook his head. So I began. I skipped the anatomy and physiology lesson, figuring the *Hustler* magazines that I had recently found stashed in the ceiling of the old carriage house had provided enough of the visuals.

Then I talked softly and comfortingly and fatheringly about men and women and lust and respect and masturbation and contraception and, yes, I even threw in a fallopian tube or two, pausing every so often to see if he wanted to "share" something with me or ask a question that would really launch our bonding experience and let him know that sex and sexual thoughts were healthy and wonderful aspects of growing up. Cael sat there, absorbing my every word like a sponge, eyes fixed on some distant object over that same left shoulder.

Forty-seven minutes later I had done the complete Masters and Johnson introductory lecture series, and though it hadn't gone quite as I planned, I felt pretty pleased with myself. I stuffed an Oreo in my smiling mouth, slapped my stomach like George C. Scott in *Dr. Strangelove*, and crooned, "That pretty much covers it, Cael. Any questions now?"

He lurched back from his stupor and glared at me, just like he did when I woke him each morning for school. "Anything?"

"Yeah, Dad"—he looked up and paused—"I have been wonderin' about somethin'...." My heart fluttered. My hands tingled. I was prepared to tell him everything. Everything. He said, "How do you think the Giants are gonna do this year?"

THE ZEN DRIVING SCHOOL

Artless parallel parking

Don't think: Look!
—WITTGENSTEIN

One day you boost them up that first mountainous step onto a yellow school bus to go to kindergarten, and the next day they come home wearing earphones and asking for a ride to the Motor Vehicle office to get a learner's permit.

"You're too young."

"I'm sixteen!"

"No, you're not. You're in third grade. And take those things off. I can't hear you when you're listening to music."

"First of all, (anatomical expletive inaudible), I'm a sophomore in high school, and second, (character expletive inaudible), I'm the one listening to the music, not you, and I can hear you perfectly well . . . although I sometimes wish I couldn't!"

And so it goes. Being the one ahead—as another Zen koan goes—it always seems that you're one or two steps (or grades) behind. But reality is reality, although in this instance reality is nonreality (more on that later), and soon after that stunning bit of psychodrama where you realize that your baby is old enough

to drive the family Jeep, you find yourself strapped into the pas-
senger seat making outlandishly paranoid statements like "You
must assume that everyone on the road is an idiot or a drunk or
a psychotic murderer out to cross the center line and kill you.
That's defensive driving."

Every experienced driver knows in his or her mechanical
soul that good driving has little to do with proper technique.
Technique is mostly learned on that first white-knuckled Saturday that you and your third grader in a sophomore's body drive
around the high school parking lot or down the deserted country lane. After that, it's all about attaining a kind of nonthinking
communication with the two-thousand-pound metal beast that
can hurtle you through space at speeds beyond what the original
Maker designed the human body to travel.

Good drivers perform, they don't think. Consider all the times
you've zoned out for thirty or forty minutes while driving from
one city to the next, absorbed in memory or fantasy or in recon-
structing the argument you just lost: you kept the car at a reasonable speed and on the right side of the road, you signaled,
you made turns, you braked, and somehow you got where you
were going.

Bad drivers think. They drive as if they are perpetually taking
their road tests with Big Bertha and her Designed-for-Failure
Clipboard. As every experienced driver knows, it is much harder
to keep the car within the lines if you're thinking about keeping
within the lines than if your mind is a blank.

So learning to drive is not about learning to drive. It is about
attaining a state of unconscious oneness with the machine. And
so it should be perfect for teenagers, who rarely if ever have a
driving thought in their heads.

Yet, put a teenager in the driver's seat, and that is precisely
when she or he first experiences focused thought. About the key
to ignition. About the cosmic order of transmission. About the
mirrors to the immediate past. About backing up to go forward.
About obstacles in the road of life. About the way to gain do-

minion over the tape player and open the window and attain the right elbow angle of calmness and make the sounds in your brain resemble words, all the while trying intently to keep the car in between the lines.

The consequence of all that thinking is situational paralysis. What should be reflexive action in response to the stop sign up ahead is not action but thoughtful indecision, such as when to brake—or not to brake—for the red light, until the Zen teacher has been completely un-Zenned, screaming, arms up across his face, right foot jammed into the pedalless floor, "Not the gas, you fool, the brake! The brake! THE BRAKE!"

The key to getting teenagers to stop thinking while driving is to talk nonstop the entire agonizing driving lesson for no other reason than to get them to listen to you, not to their own inner voices. I also keep the driving lessons short so that their self-contained thoughts don't leach out and confuse me to the point that I lose my edge of pure perceptions and start grabbing for the wheel.

As for parallel parking and other such esoteric skills, the fewer mechanical tips the better. We go through the process several times together and then I tell them everything is done by feel. By visualization. Pull up to the car ahead of the vacant space, line up the steering wheels, and see yourself moving the car back into the space, six inches from the curb. And then do it. Then I get out of the car and leave them to their own process of achieving mindlessness.

Same thing with learning to drive standard transmissions, although I advise doing this after your hot-rodders have already passed the driver's test on an automatic. Show the neophytes what to do, go through the bucking motions a few times, and then have an out-of-car experience. Give them the keys and tell them to find their transcendent spirit. Then stand back and watch as they buck and stall and grind the gears and ride the clutch until they're out of sight.

And when they return later on driving like old pros, yell at them for going too fast.

WHERE'S PAPA?

The importance of being in the picture

> *Be here now.*
> —RAM DASS

A hazy one-hundred-degree day. Around four o'clock the small town pool is beginning to fill up with dads. Young dads, old dads, fat dads, black dads, white dads . . . you get the picture. Some are tossing kids in the thick air above the chlorinated blue. Some stand at ease in genital-deep water like sergeants instructing new recruits. Some do laps, seals with goggles and nose plugs. Some never make it to the water; they go right to the frayed beach chair and hide behind the paper.

One thing we have in common is that we all look like dads. You can't buy this fleshy look anywhere. We also sound like dads, barking at kids to settle down, demanding change as we hand out a buck to buy a Bomb Pop, soothing a toddler who has just scraped her knee. There's nothing remarkable here except that there is nothing remarkable here.

New Paltz is a nice place to be a kid—and a dad. The mountains, the college, and a funky main street provide extraordinary playing fields beyond all the green parks and playgrounds. Children here are known as much by who they are as by the name their family has made for itself in local lore.

I tried to imagine on that intensely hot summer day—Bay and Elizabeth in the shallow section, Clover lounging on a blanket with friends, Danny tossing a ball with Keith and Jessie—what would happen if a group of teenagers formed a "whirlpool" here in New Paltz, as some boys apparently did several years ago in the Crotona Pool in the South Bronx: locking arms and moving in circles across the pool, chanting song lyrics, laughing, surrounding a frightened girl, and fondling her.

It didn't take much imagination, though. The lifeguards would be blowing whistles like crazy and jerking their college-educated thumbs to order the out-of-control mob out of the pool. Six foot six head lifeguard Dave O'Neill would scream bloody murder and throw the group out of the park—maybe for a week, probably for the entire summer. He'd threaten to call the police. And, frankly, that would be the easiest part of the ordeal for most of the errant boys.

Before they made it safely away from Dave—and Bonnie and Rich and Mike and all the other outraged big brothers and sisters who sling whistles like guns at Moriello Pool—the whirlpool gang would have to answer to the fuming dads storming their way, venomous men with bulging veins in their necks who would appear two earth-shattering steps away from an angry coronary.

I could see dads grown suddenly enormous with massive hands on love-handled hips glaring down into the terrified eyes of their suddenly skinny boys; dads with their thick fingers clasped around the back of boys' chicken necks, pushing them behind the bath house; dads—red dads, yellow dads, white dads, black dads (you get the picture)—index fingers jabbing bony chests.

I could feel the boys' silky backs rubbed up against rough cinder block walls. I could hear the boys crying. I shuddered at the sight of those wrathful fathers, mouths open like dark cauldrons of fire, bellowing the way that dads have bellowed at their bad boys throughout the ages.

And then I looked around at all the dads planted around our local pool and wondered where the fathers of the whirlpooling boys had been that summer. And if they could not be there, what about the uncles and the big brothers? Why wasn't someone right there to calm the roiling waters and save those boys from themselves?

When I closed my eyes, though, all I could see was a circle of panoramic photographs, crowded pools across the country swirling with thousands of perilous eddies, abandoned boys linking hands with each other and singing away their confusion, anger, and pain. And at the center of each of those whirlpools was a terrified little girl—some father's daughter—whose dad had forsaken her to a world where boys never learn to grow up to be men.

As Ram Dass says, Be here now! Now! Presence is all.

SEEKING IDENTITY

What makes Danny run . . . and get busted

> *Trying to define yourself is like trying to bite your own teeth.*
>
> —ALAN WATTS

Whatever psychological issues the fifth (or sixth or seventh) child in a big family may face, there is one distinct advantage for kids on the lower end of the pecking order: from the very beginnings of consciousness, they've seen enough real life to harbor no illusions about domestic bliss. They've had front-row booster seats for some historic family battles and by puberty should know how to navigate the treacherous waters between parents and teenagers.

Take Danny, our current misunderstood sixteen-year-old. He's had a lifetime to observe the assembled crimes and punishments of his older siblings. He's seen Cael busted for partying while the parents are away; he's peeked at Nancy being collared for arriving long past curfew—and he knows all about the midnight call from the local police. No doubt he's contemplated how Addie deftly and sometimes defiantly eluded punishment for crimes worthy of long-term incarceration. And he's been mindfully attentive as Clover learned the value of going about

her misdeeds in a quiet and uncontentious manner—and, in doing so, got away with practically everything.

So, life for Danny should be a teenage cakewalk. With all
that knowledge and experience laid out behind him, Danny's
existence should be grounded in groundlessness. Yet . . .

Beginning with the secret stash of two warm beers and a couple of stale Marlboros we found in the storage shed of the cottage in Hatteras when he was thirteen, and moving on through
what has seemed like a monthly smorgasbord of petty family
misdemeanors, Dan the Man has probably spent more weekend
nights incarcerated at home than any of his brothers and sisters—and perhaps all of them combined.

Danny's life could be read as a minor tragedy, not only because he seems to get caught all the time, but because I know
that he's probably done less "bad" stuff than his supposedly innocent sisters. (I'm still finding out about the indiscretions they
committed while living under our "jurisdiction.")

There are two nontranscendent reasons why Danny has gotten
busted more often than his siblings. One is that although I enjoy
teenagers immensely—I love the way they knock over the furniture of our lives as they move toward adulthood; I love their
often unlovable music, their unwearable clothes, their unintelli-
gible language, their utterly selfish selflessness—I have no illusions about their innocence.

Nor does Patti. As his four siblings preceded Danny through
the gates of pubescent angst, Patti and I were not hiding under
the quilts with our hands over our ears. We've seen it all, or at
least most of it.

But, we can't take all the credit for Danny's well-grounded life.

The second reason for the oxymoronic nature of Danny's
predicament has been his search for identity in this big con-
glomerate of a family. As Alan Watts understood so well, trying to define yourself is both the simplest and most impossible
of undertakings; and, if I may add something to the Zen master's observation, trying to define yourself in the context of a

big family makes the whole process even simpler and more inaccessible.

Cael was the Cassanova of the family, Nancy the mathematical Einstein, Addie the clone of her mom, and Clover a graceful equestrienne. Danny, too, sought not only an identity from the outside world but a special recognition among his siblings. As such, Danny inadvertently became the James Dean Rebel Without Much Cause in our brood, the one with a good heart who always gets himself into trouble. Consequently, he has always dropped bread crumbs along his felonious path. And while his older siblings might laugh at his ongoing troubles, with each new indictment they've also nodded their heads and said to themselves, "Hey, the little twerp has some backbone. He's all right, after all."

And he is.

A KEG OF BEER, LOAFING ON THE COUCH, AND THE LIVING ROOM RUG OUT ON THE LAWN

Axiom: When parents are gone, teenagers will party

I'm seventeen: I'm supposed to lie to you!
—C. Lewis

No sense being coy about it, there is an axiom of family life with teenagers that must be understood by all parents in order for them to attain the next level of spiritual development (i.e., freedom without fear):

When Parents Are Gone, Teenagers Will Party.

This requires no psychological analysis, no social commentary, no spiritual homilies, just a simple story.

When Patti and I told the kids over dinner that we were all going to the beach at Montauk for the long Columbus Day weekend, everyone was instantly excited. Everyone, that is, except Cael. He fell into a grumbling despair, barely finishing his meal with that look of utter disgust that only a teenager can affect.

Actually, I understood his predicament. Like any seventeen-year-old, he was as horrified at the prospect of spending two nights in a couple of mildewy hotel rooms with his five brothers and sisters (Elizabeth was not yet born) as he was humiliated at the vision of walking around in public with giggly girls, a doofy boy, a smelly baby, and two parents who could embarrass a rock.

I actually don't remember whether we took pity on him and decided he was old enough to stay by himself, or if he moaned so insistently about the boredom that awaited him that he wore us down and we relented against our better judgment. It doesn't really matter.

After I extracted several solemn promises from him that there would be no parties ("Dad . . . ," he said, voice dripping with annoyance at my lack of faith), Patti gave him a nonstop lecture on the (two) dos and (sixty-seven) don'ts of staying home alone. Then we gave him a cross-indexed three-page list of emergency numbers; stocked the refrigerator as if we were going away for two months; and Nancy, Addie, Clover, Danny, Bay, Patti, and I left for two and a half beach-filled days at the charmingly downscale Eastdeck Motel in Montauk.

"I know he's having a party," Patti said as we walked the beach on Saturday.

I assured her he wasn't. "He told me he wouldn't. Cael does a lot of things but he doesn't lie."

And so I instantly achieved the Zen state of pure cognitive dissonance when we drove up the long driveway two days later and saw the living room oriental rug spread out on the front lawn. I knew but I didn't know.

Cael met us with as goofy a grin as you'd ever want to see and, after all the yelling and screaming died down, admitted that he'd had a *few* friends over and that the bubble of beer that they had somehow gotten had accidentally fallen off the table and soaked the rug.

Two hours later Patti spoke to Alice Tenuto (our closest neighbor through the woods—about a quarter of a mile away) who said she *heard* the party going all night *and* later found out that practically the entire senior class was there.

Cael was grounded for the rest of his life, and Patti and I

agreed that we would never again leave a teenager home alone for more than a couple of hours.

Except, six months later, which was several months after he had been "paroled" for something akin to good behavior, Patti and I again made plans for another family weekend trip. And of course Cael didn't want to join us, which prompted an emergency meeting at the highest levels of family governance to review public policy. Patti was skeptical, but I argued that since he was properly chastened and punished by the rug-in-the-yard fiasco, it would be a real statement of faith in his character if we trusted him enough to let him stay home.

That evening Cael and I sat down and had a father-son man-to-man heart-to-heart mano-a-mano talk about trust and maturity and the meaning of family. (I don't know what the last had to do with the first two, but I toss it out periodically if I don't know what else to say.)

And Cael nodded soberly and sincerely as if he agreed with every word I had spoken. At the end I said, "Look me in the eye and promise that you're not going to have a party, Cael. That's all I need." I didn't even drop my voice the fatherly three octaves. We were pals now, men of the world.

He looked me right in the eye and said, "I'm not going to have a party, Dad." And we hugged, men of the world together.

Of course you know where this is going. And of course he had a party. And although they didn't soak the living room rug, the big jerk used no-wax floor polish to clean up the pine wood floors, thus creating a dull, thick, hazy finish all over the house. There were spaghetti strands stuck on the kitchen wall, wrinkled sheets on every bed in the house, the heavy clink of beer bottles in the trash.

So, there I was right in his downturned face, veins bursting in my neck as I rose to the essence of my paternal rage: "Worst of all, Cael, worst of all, is the fact that you lied to me! You looked me in the eye and promised you would not have a party."

And he looked me in the eye and said without a hint of deception, "I'm seventeen, Dad: I'm supposed to lie to you!"

Ah, truth.

So Cael was grounded once again for the rest of his life, and Patti and I swore we'd never again leave a teenager home alone overnight. And we pretty much kept our word until Nancy and Addie ("The girls would never lie to us like that!") had an extravaganza several years later that apparently rivaled a Grateful Dead concert—and, as a nice little touch, tripped and poked a hole in the wall with the vacuum cleaner while cleaning up.

THE EMPTY NEST

What happens when they leave for college (and can't come home on weekends)

> When you do something, you should burn yourself completely, like a good bonfire, leaving no trace of yourself.
> —SHUNRYU SUZUKI

Many parents we know want their children to choose colleges near home. Not so with us. At the risk of sounding a little cold-hearted, we encourage our kids to go at least a state or two away; far enough so that they can't come home on a whim every Friday afternoon.

When I'm taking the high road on these matters I say that in order to find themselves, kids need to leave what is safe and comfortable and predictable. As Chogyam Trungpa says in *Shambhala: The Sacred Path of the Warrior*, "This is your world! You can't not look. . . . Open your eyes. Don't blink, and look, look—look further." Beyond state lines.

On the low road you might hear me say, "Your salad days are over, kid. We love you dearly, kid, but eighteen years of laundry, dirty plates, strange friends, and outstretched palms is enough. It's time to hit the road."

So Cael went all the way down to Tallahassee, Florida, and Nancy flew off to Chapel Hill, North Carolina, and Addie zoomed away to State College, Pennsylvania, and Clover joined Nancy in Chapel Hill. Nobody's closer than four and a half hours by train, plane, or automobile.

In our family there's a two-step process by which one prepares to leave home. Step one occurs years before freshman orientation and involves moving your teenage self and everything you own (and have been able to steal from your brothers and sisters) up to the attic, where there are two bedrooms and a space that might be loosely termed a den with a TV, VCR, and a remarkably uncomfortable dusty couch.

There is no bathroom up there, and it's a three-story walk-up, and it's frigidly cold in winter and suffocatingly hot in summer, and the rooms are more cell-like than roomy, and the rain on the roof sounds like pebbles dropped from the heavens, but the attic is the closest thing to heaven that a teenager can imagine without paying rent. Close the door from the second-floor hall and you're safe from meddling parents and annoying little kids and the embarrassing inanities of family life.

As the oldest in the family, Cael and Nancy staked their claims to the "loft" when we built the house years ago. There was no protest from the other kids; as in most families, there are rights and privileges that go along with age. (Danny was reminded of the hierarchical nature of family life when we were all together last summer on Hatteras. Everyone piled into the Jeep and Danny was "ordered" by the older crew into the "way back" with Bay and Elizabeth. He was nothing short of incredulous: "I'm sixteen! I don't sit with the little kids!" Cael's reply was brief: "As long as we're around, you're number five. Now get in the back." Then he turned to Addie with a sneer and said, "He'll probably be sitting in the way back when he's thirty-six and married with kids.")

So, at the very moment that Cael was closing the lid on the last suitcase to bring to college, Addie was down on the second floor plotting her territorial grab. And as the last of his bags were dragged down two flights and out to the car, the implements of takeover were being stealthily transported up to the attic.

Before he was even out of the house, his bed was dismantled and dragged out of the room.

Addie did make the trek downstairs to give him a kiss and a hug good-bye, and she did stand and wave from the front porch as he left. But then she raced—two steps at a time—to the hot attic paradise that by rights was already hers. And with his body scent still lingering in the air, she painted him out of existence. In pink.

Two hours later, any reminder or reminiscent sense of his time and presence in the room was completely gone. In a form of familial alchemy, it had been transformed completely into Addie's room. (And Addie's room on the second floor was taken over by Danny, who bolted from the room he shared with Bay as if his life depended on it.)

When Cael came home from college that first Thanksgiving and found no traces of his former self up on the third floor—and saw Addie standing symbolically in the doorway with an imaginary Winchester cradled in her arms—he got the picture and took up temporary residence in the tiny sewing room on the second floor. And, as if that wasn't humbling enough, two years later he was relegated to sharing the bunk bed with Danny or any available couch after Nancy left for UNC and Clover immediately planted her flag and her army of ten thousand stuffed animals in the attic room next to Addie.

Nancy, who had observed Addie's expression of manifest destiny, quickly claimed rights to the sewing room before Cael got home for Christmas vacation.

And so it goes. Just as in life, when you go, you hardly leave a trace behind. Everything keeps moving. Everything is in flux. Aside from the photographs all over the walls of this big home— and the memories of the children who grew up here—all of which suggests an immutable sense of place, there are no monuments here, no childhood sanctums, no historic designations.

And, paraphrasing Walter Cronkite, because it is always that way, that is the way it is.

7

Nanto (or Hard-to-Penetrate Koan) and Teenage Girls

ZEN DAD, UN-ZEN BOYFRIENDS

The pimply faced boys who show up at your door

> *The quieter you become the more you can hear.*
> —RAM DASS

He shuffles his feet, glances up at the ceiling, coughs, jams his hands in his pockets. Snatches a peek at me out of the corner of his eye. A halting minute later he's trying man-talk with me—cars, boxing, fishing, money, his plans after high school or college.

But I keep my distance. I don't talk much. As he and my daughter finally leave, I offer a low-key "Have a good time." He knows what I mean, though. He knows I'll be staring out the window, watching how he drives away.

I can hear him say to her later, his voice soft at the edges, "Your father doesn't like me."

And I imagine her telling him, "Don't be ridiculous. Of course he does. He likes all my friends."

But she's wrong this time. The barest truth is that I don't like the boy, even though there's a very good chance I liked him last month—that is, the day before he started dating my daughter. In fact, odds are good that I treated him just like I do any of the boys who come around to visit. I welcome them in. I offer them sodas. I laugh at their jokes. I put a hand on their shoulder as a coach or a friendly uncle might do.

Not this one, though. In the timespan of a quick kiss on the lips, he's suddenly found himself, in effect, in a back room sitting on a hard wooden chair with a light over his head. He's suddenly got something to prove to me that has nothing to do with a charming grin or a firm handshake or an intelligent remark or a game-winning goal. I'm not impressed with flowers or jewelry or poetry.

Everybody knows why he wants me to like him: he's attracted to my daughter, and one way or another, I'm an important man in her life. He wants me to like him *only* because he wants her to like him so much that she'll give her heart to him. He wants her to love him.

And while love may indeed be the essence of life—the alpha and the omega—it's also true that nothing in this life can do more damage to a person than lost or abusive love. Everybody also knows that. So any boy who comes to take her heart is going to be seen by me at first as an intruder, a threat, a dangerous snake the moment he first slips through the door.

Frankly, it doesn't much matter to me if his hair goes down to his butt or is clipped marine-close to the scalp. It also doesn't really matter if he's got a nose ring or a class ring, a BMW or a bicycle, a leather jacket or a tweed sport coat. He's come to steal her heart. So he's dangerous.

Love and affection and companionship and sex are all a part of life, so I won't—and can't—protect her from any of it. Any of it. I haven't been and won't ever be a warden to any of my children, but I am going to watch him as insistently as a circling hawk.

And the one thing I'm going to watch most carefully is the way that he treats her when he thinks I'm not watching. The biggest mistake any boy can make—and it's the very one too many of them believe is their right—is to try to be her protector. It's simply not his job; it's mine, and it's the very one that I have been working to walk away from since she was small enough to be cradled in one arm.

I've held her for hours while she burned up with fever; I've rushed her to emergency rooms with broken bones; I've confronted teachers who have hurt her with their words; I've tried to put my arm around her quivering shoulders when some boy broke up with her. I've grounded her when she's done wrong; I've said no a million times. Always to protect her. That's been my job.

Ironically, these Prince Valiants are always fawning at first. Overly attentive and overwhelmingly considerate, they start off treating their girlfriends like princesses who must be shaded from the harsh light of daily life. Some even lack the perspective to keep quiet about how well they'll take care of them.

As soon as I hear the conspiratorially macho "I'll have her in by . . . ," I know there's going to be trouble. And it will be in the form of a jealous boy slowly growing more moody, manipulative, and demanding, eventually becoming a ridiculously macho caricature of his own misguided notions of maleness. At some point his desperation might even become a dangerous weapon.

So I keep my distance. I watch very carefully. I listen.

And not until the moment I see that he *truly* cares for her do I begin to stop watching. When I see a smile of real happiness on my daughter's face when he shows up at the door—not the relief that comes of desperation or fear—I invite him in. When I can hear the joyous sound of them talking, playing, arguing, and laughing as equals, I put my hand on his shoulder.

When he wants to be her friend, not mine, then we'll be friends. Then I'll talk.

POCKETFUL OF GIRL STUFF

The mysterious disappearance of the old man's clothes

> *The Buddha taught that all things, including his castle, are essentially impermanent and as soon as man tries to possess them they slip away.*
>
> —ALAN WATTS

At first, most fathers think it's cute: you pick up your thirteen-year-old daughter at the Middle School dance and find her wearing your favorite blue button-down oxford shirt, sleeves rolled heavily just below the elbow, tails at her knobby knees, a grown-up smirk on her beautiful baby face.

"Nice shirt," you say slyly, walking to the parking lot.

She giggles. "Daaa-deeee . . . you weren't home when I was getting ready—and it looked great on me—and I didn't think you'd mind—and I didn't get any stains on it. . . ."

You don't say much because there's nothing to say and you'd be a fool to try to get a word in edgewise anyway. You just smile like the fool she's playing you for. Then she plants the seed of future incursions into your closet and drawers that will eventually leave you naked and bereft: "You're not mad, are you, Daddy?"

Of course you're not mad. You're actually flattered for reasons beyond your understanding—and, really, she looks so cute.

You laugh and take her delicate little hand in yours and, in effect, give her the keys to the wardrobe. "Not at all, baby girl. Not at all."

In fact, this is bliss: your little girl in your big manly shirt and you acting like the most understanding, hippest dad in town. For a moment you sense some inarticulated danger and revert to the authoritarian "Just let me know when you're borrowing a shirt or something, so I won't think it's lost." Whatever that means. And with that, you think that's the end of it.

It's not.

The next thing I knew, Nancy was fifteen, a little too womanly to be cute anymore, and on her back was a shirt that I vaguely remembered owning but hadn't seen in months. "Is that mine?" I asked like the doddering fool she knew I was capable of being.

"No," she said with unsettling conviction for a girl who was lying through her teeth, "but I think Addie's wearing your sweatshirt." And I turned around to discover that Addie was indeed thirteen and looking as cute as a button (whatever *that* means) in my extra-large Florida State sweatshirt, cuffs down over her fingers, stretched out waistband below her knees. And I was ineffably flattered—and sidetracked—once again, just as I would be enchanted two years later by the sight of Clover dressed up in my Paul Simon *Still Crazy After All These Years* concert T-shirt.

At that point I began to think that perhaps I was crazy because it seemed that I was seeing my clothes—or clothes that I thought I might have once owned—on teenage girls all around this town.

One night I swore I saw Addie's friend Anita in what might have been my North Carolina sweatshirt; and the next week I'm sure I spotted Jessica, Clover's best friend, in a flannel shirt that I hadn't worn in at least two years. Then there was the girl whose name I did not know strolling down Main Street in my Rodanthe Surfshop hat.

But nothing prepared me for the singular experience of arriving at the Listorts' house one night to find Nancy's friend Cynthia wearing my plaid boxers!

I was speechless. What could I say? *What are you doing in my shorts?* I don't think Cynthia had a clue that they were mine. The way these things go, she might not have even known that she got them through Nancy—or Addie. It's quite possible that Anita was wearing my underwear and she lent it to Kristen or Tiffany and one of them lent the shorts to Cynthia.

At that singular moment, my drawers full but completely devoid of me, it seemed to me that I achieved a Zen state of true emptiness.

But I was wrong. My moment of immortality came soon after discovering a favorite jacket (which I forgot I owned) under a six-foot pile of towels on the floor of Clover's room. I was so happy to find it that I didn't yell at her for stealing my clothes again—or for the pile of twenty-three (yes, twenty-three) towels that left the rest of the family drying off with washcloths.

And the next morning I drove off in my newly rediscovered favorite hipster-poet jacket to teach my advanced placement English classes over in the quaint village of Millbrook. When I arrived at the 140-year-old Thorne Building, the old heating system had not quite brought the classrooms up to sixty degrees, so I kept my jacket on while teaching the class.

Midway through the lesson, as I paced back and forth in front of the room, I reached into the pocket and felt something unusual. Something cylindrical. It was hard but covered with paper. I had no idea what it could be.

So, in between some well-chosen insights into the extreme narcissism of Othello and the nature of jealousy, I pulled the alien object out of the depths of the pocket and . . . the room erupted in soul-shaking laughter as I stood there with a slender Tampax in my hand.

In that epiphanic moment I saw everything—the past, the present, the future—and knew in my soul that there was no possible explanation that would do justice to the curious vision of a forty-something teacher standing before a group of high school seniors with a feminine hygiene product in his outstretched hand.

My red-faced silence was an acknowledgment that all things are essentially impermanent, clothing as well as embarrassment.

ARE YOU SAYING I'M FAT?

Teenage girls and their unholy relationship with food

It is an ordinary thing to be holy. We do such extra-ordinary things not to be.

—JAMES HAZARD

Clover looks in a trifold mirror at the department store and frowns. Then she turns around and cranes her head over her neck like a gazelle, gets up on her toes, and mutters, "My butt's too big for this dress."

I'm looking in the same mirror—at the very same moment—and I don't see a big butt. In fact, I don't see a big anything. Mostly, I see this gorgeous, slim-hipped, electric eighteen-year-old girl, a vision of budding womanhood—the girl voted "Best Physique" by the PC-conscious 1995 senior class at New Paltz High School. Not "Biggest Butt."

I asked myself a question to which I already knew the answer: "How could two relatively reasonable people be looking at the same reflected vision and see two distinct and contradictory realities?"

And the answer was at once far too serious and far too ridiculous to answer adequately.

Suffice it to say that because teenage girls are, by cosmic design, narcissists who see the world solely in terms of themselves, they find themselves at the merciless hands of anyone and everyone (boys, men, teen magazines, advertisers) who have a personal stake in making them feel too big. Boys, who are also narcissists, have the exact opposite problem; they see themselves as smaller than they really are and consequently must go around proving how big they are.

I knew the answer, not because I have a great insight into the cosmos of teenage perception but because Nancy and Addie preceded Clover through the valley of the shadow of psychic fat—and, a long ways back, I remember my high school girl-friend Judy at Jones Beach covering her lower half with a towel because her rather compelling thighs were "too fat." (One doesn't easily forget cognitive dissonance like that.)

Nancy, like Clover, was your run-of-the-mill teenage narcissist who saw rolls of blubber in the most unlikely places. She also opened my eyes to another paradox of parenting: a clueless father takes his daughter to lunch, spends hundreds of dollars on clothing she doesn't even need, and somehow, it turns out to be a miserable and demoralizing experience.

Addie, however, brought body misperception to the level of an art form during her teenage years. I don't want to make light of a very serious problem in our society that has led to untold numbers of young women starving and purging themselves to death, but at the less self-destructive levels, there is a Zen resonance in the way teenage girls perceive their weight in the world.

At sixteen Addie not only knew that mirrors lie, she knew how to look through them to see the real truth about her supposedly flabby body. Watching a girl with no body fat do stomach crunches and other painful forms of penance in front of the TV to ward off cellulite and flab made me realize how serious her quest for a perfectly thin body had become. (For the uninformed, stomach crunches are agonizing exercises designed for narcissists of both sexes who want to achieve what is commonly known as a six-pack: a hard and taut belly, which, when flexed, produces a six-ripple effect from the rib cage down to the Calvin Klein waistband.)

However, the awareness of this perfect absurdity came later on. I was innocently walking down the stairs one afternoon and saw Addie sitting against the wall, her feet up on the banister, talking on the phone with her friend Jana.

I suppose I assumed naively that she would just swivel around and let me pass. She didn't. It's possible that she hadn't noticed me towering above her on the narrow step, though it was difficult to imagine that a conversation with Jana could be that riveting. So, all I said was, "Excuse me."

Moving nothing but her eyeballs, she glared at me as if I had just said the most insulting thing a man ever said to a woman. "What?"

"I said, 'Excuse me.' "

"Are you saying I'm fat?" she scowled, not missing a beat.

Stuck on the steps, I stuttered in disbelief, "There's not an ounce of fat on your body, Adelyn, and, besides, what has that got to do with my trying to come down the stairs?"

She swiveled around, stood up, and muttered, "Like you don't know. . . ." Then she pressed her body flat against the wall, leaving a space wide enough for a Mack truck to drive through.

From that point on I understood that it's virtually impossible to argue with teenage misperception. You just give in and wait it out.

That is why, years later on the shopping trip with Clover, I was able to view her megabottom from a more cosmic perspective.

I simply agreed with her, and we went to another store in the mall where they stock dresses that hide one's big butt.

ZEN AND THE
TEENAGE GIRL

*How to say one thing and mean
something totally different*

In every truth the opposite is equally true.
—HERMANN HESSE

Addie tilts her head. A smirk sneaks across her lips. "You know, I just realized that I can do whatever I want. You don't really have control over me anymore."

She is eighteen, nearing the end of her senior year in high school. She's full of herself: smart, charming, athletic, pretty. In her purse are the keys to a beat-up old Plymouth. On her arm, a boyfriend who makes her parents uneasy. In her folder, an acceptance letter from Penn State. Everything is perfect.

I smile, a standard parental stall, but I know that what she says is true. After children reach a certain age, parents exert only the most superficial control over their destinies. We may continue to inform or lecture them about acceptable behavior, and insist that certain rules be maintained in the home, but when they walk out the door each morning, they make their own choices. They lead their own lives.

Of course I wish it were different; it's a perilous world out there, and part of me would like to be Addie's Schwarzeneggersize Jiminy Cricket, poised over her shoulder in the same watchful way that I was when she was four and learning to ride her two-wheeler. But the simple truth is I cannot watch over my beautiful daughter every moment of the day, just as I could not watch Cael and Nancy when they were seniors, just as I will not be able to watch over Clover, Danny, Bay, and Elizabeth Bayou-Grace when it's their time of ascendancy.

I tell Addie all that in a soft, fatherly voice, admittedly feeling more than a little smug that I have come up with a response that is steeped in ageless parental wisdom.

She's not satisfied, though. There is more to this challenge than simply her freedom, and I simply don't get it. "I meant that even if you ground me, I don't really have to listen to you anymore." There is a wrinkle of nervousness around the smirk. I see my bold little toddler sixteen years earlier with that same expression.

"Yes, but . . . there are limits. . . ." I'm not sure what I mean by that, but limits seems a good concept at the moment.

"I mean, truthfully, Dad, what are you going to do if I don't accept the grounding, throw me out of the house? You'd never throw me out of the house, would you?" She glances sideways for the answer.

While scurrying around behind my glassy eyes, searching for some safe wall against which to back up, I see finally that she's not talking about rules at all but rather something like "This is all moving too quickly. I'm supposed to leave everything behind in just a few months. So, I just want to know whether it's possible that I can stay home and behave like an impudent child and still be treated like an adult?"

Conventional Western wisdom (and some subterranean memories of my father speaking to me on the same subject) tell me to say, "No, you can't have your cake and eat it, too." You're either on or off the bus. A boss or an employee. A child or an adult. Set limits. Be consistent. Right is right.

Yet, accompanying my children on their journey through the

dark acned tunnel of adolescence, I have acquired a kind of night vision that allows me to see that nothing is exactly as it seems. Indeed, the parental highway for me has been rather foggy and paradoxical: wrong is sometimes right and right is often wrong. And at the heart of all those contradictions is the most unsettling one of all: that while my children belong to me, they are not mine exclusively.

I don't ever want Addie to think that she is not welcome in my home, yet I don't want her to think that I will allow her to take my home away from me.

So when she asks if I'd ever throw her out of the house, I stutter out a windy yes and then follow with a grunting no and then a quavering yes and no. Finally, in an unintentional paradigm of my own ignorant wisdom: "I don't know what I'd do, Adelyn."

She frowns, disappointed that I haven't concocted a concrete, documentable answer of the on-or-off-the-bus variety. She wants to know whether it's Tough Love Dad or Saint Steven the Martyr. She wants a statement of fact, a simple list of rights and wrongs, the kind that is retrieved from someone's kindergarten teacher or from a wise Jewish grandmother or from some postdoctoral fellow at Harvard interviewed on *Donahue*: good, sane, logical advice on how to be perfectly happy and perfectly protected from the vagaries of an imperfect world.

Stranded in the swirling darkness of this cosmically indefinable problem, all that comes to mind is an aphorism spoken by a man who is neither a Zen master nor a parent: "Love your children most when they least deserve it." Jerry Sherman, a wonderful earth science teacher at Millbrook High School, offered that simple truth nearly ten years ago at a graduation ceremony I attended. And I knew instantly it was the smartest thing I had ever heard. Love is simply not something to be earned or bartered.

So I don't answer Addie's question, saying only that I love her with all my heart, that I will always be her father, in life and in death, reaching across to hold her close, to breathe in that extraordinary essence, just as I did when she was a terrible two and as easy to embrace as a summer morning.

When we part, she presses her lips together and turns toward the safety of her cluttered bedroom, a room Danny will claim as his the day she moves out. Before the door closes, though, she turns with a sad smile and says, "I wasn't asking if you loved me. . . ."

I nod, but it's not to her, it's to Jerry Sherman, who knows the beautiful answer to the question nobody asks.

OUTSIDE THE GARDEN

One night before Nancy graduated from high school . . .

> *We have it completely backwards: instead of being very strict with little children and gradually opening the gates of freedom as they grow older, we give little children far too much freedom and then try desperately to rein them in when they get older and wilder.*
>
> —PATRICIA HENDERSON LEWIS

Nancy was born on my twenty-seventh birthday. I'm not sure if that explains why my memories sometimes seem to get spliced with hers, but her senior year in high school turned on reels of remembrances that had been lost for decades.

In my home movie of the fifties and sixties, Roslyn Heights, New York, was a place of paramount comfort and security. I awoke each morning to two parents, glass bottles of milk outside the front door, a Buick Roadmaster in the garage, and, of course, a perfect little lawn bounded by two other perfect little lawns that encapsulated two other two-parent families who drove big American cars and drank milk every day.

I stumbled happily enough from the I. U. Willets Road Elementary School all the way through Wheatley High without a thought to the good or evil in the world. My innocence was somehow preserved by an insulating layer of Sunday morning bagels, stuffed cabbage, cheek-pinching aunts, a pretty girlfriend, membership in the elite Varsity Club, and an Earl

Sheib–green '56 Ford. All was well with my Donna Reed world.

So it was like the film snapped near the end of my senior year at Wheatley when a classmate, Alan Ibanez, wrote in my best friend's yearbook: "To Richard, one of the good Jews . . . ," the celluloid suddenly flapping, flapping, flapping, flapping, flapping . . . and the inside of my head instantly going blank.

And in the darkness of my shaken soul, I immediately realized three things that I had never before considered:

1. That other people saw me as a Jew first and then as a person.
2. That it was generally considered a bad thing to be a Jew.
3. That it might be a dangerous world out there for Jews.

By the time the lights went back on, I had already left my safe, green, weed-free suburban childhood behind. I walked across the stage, accepted my diploma, and sat back down amid the congratulations of friends and oppressors, right and left. Two months later I left for college with my eyes permanently opened.

So I thought about Alan Ibanez again a few days before Nancy would graduate from high school and it was her turn to enter the "real world." Though she was far more sophisticated than I was at eighteen, I suspected that she was just as naive as to the vicissitudes of life on this planet.

Nancy grew up in a big farmhouse in the middle of the woods with six brothers and sisters—and dogs and cats and ducks and bunnies and goats—and two parents. She spent warm summer days lying in the hammock; she wandered the cool, rocky stream near the house; she kissed her boyfriend Michael on the porch swing. She probably knew more about the profound and passionate drama of life than I did at her age, but I don't think she saw her role in the midst of it all.

The night before her graduation I lay in bed listening to the owls and peepers and the low murmur of voices out in the vine-covered gazebo. Nancy and her friends were hanging out, making the night—that is, their childhoods—last a few minutes longer, their laughter as easy as water gurgling over smooth rocks in the stream. In a breath they would all be off to college, and in the space of another breath the film about small-town life would snap for each of them. And in that darkness each would reckon with unknown oppressors, right and left.

So I wept for my baby girl. I am her father, her protector, yet I knew I could not protect her from what was to come her way. I turned on the projector of memory and recalled the feel of the fat baby in my young arms eighteen years before, the heat of her tiny breaths on my chest, the tiny fingers clinging to my shoulder. I played back the awful ache of leaving her crying at nursery school. I closed my eyes and met again Nate and Craig and Travis and Michael as they came calling at the front door to take her heart away.

I remembered it all, good and bad, real and mythologized, but I could not see where she would go when her Alan Ibanez character would appear and the film would snap and the screen would go blank.

That night I realized that Nancy (and Addie and Clover and Elizabeth after her) would have a double burden after leaving the nest: half Jew, not only would she be counted as a Jew before a person but she would be seen first and foremost in terms of her sex and her sexuality and the ways that she might serve the various self-serving needs of men. For a father, that is an undeniable—and unnerving—truth of life outside the Garden.

I was not so afraid that she would be overtaken by any one oppressor, for I knew she had the strength of her mother, but I was made fearful that evening of the awesome weight on her spirit when she finally would see that oppression is all around, right and left, above and below, ahead and behind. I grew afraid that she might someday sit down just when it is time to stand up and walk out; afraid that she would, in desperation, play a role in someone else's movie of her life.

I lay there wondering if I had done enough to point out to her what she must endure, if I had kept from her too many of the bitter truths one inevitably learns in life.

Yet when the low murmur of voices outside my window disappeared in the roar of a car engine and I heard the front door open and click shut, steps creaking as she tiptoed fearlessly up to her third-floor sanctuary without a care in the world, I gained a glimpse of what my protected childhood had done for me.

The insulated, green, predictable, bourgeois, schmaltzy Super-8 version of life that was Roslyn Heights, allowed me, if arguably little else, the certainty that it was good and proper to be who I am. If I was any less sure of myself and my rightful place on this earth—if I was the least bit scared or ashamed as too many oppressed people are in this world—I might have spent days (or years or even a lifetime) raging against a fool, trying desperately to set the world right again. And Alan Ibanez would still be my oppressor.

So that night, rather than fear that Nancy had not seen enough of the harsh world that surely awaited her, I prayed that the garden we had created would protect her well. I prayed that we had given her the same certainty in herself that I had discovered in myself as a young and innocent boy in Roslyn Heights. I prayed for her good passage.

SHE'S LEAVING HOME, BYE-BYE, PART I

Senioritis

> *Every parting gives a foretaste of death; every coming together again a foretaste of the resurrection.*
> —SCHOPENHAUER

Senior year in high school has but one transcendent purpose for young women: to provide ample time for them to grow so irritable and weary and contemptuous of everything associated with home that by spring everyone in the family is awaiting their departure with relief and gratitude.

The process is always the same: the girls spend all junior year looking forward to their time of ascendancy, and by the following summer anticipation has reached such a fever pitch that they are incapable of talking to each other without squealing.

That's as high as it gets, though. By her first day of the last year of school Nancy had already acquired the symptomatic sneer of early senioritis; by Thanksgiving she had "had it" with school and a couple of her old friends; after Christmas she gave up on homework and all household chores; and in February, afflicted with a chronic form of the malaise, she felt so claustrophobic that being in a room with the "fam" for more than fifteen minutes was sixteen minutes too many.

And thus the phrase "I gotta get outahere!" was born—and repeated so often that it became a mantra that carried us through spring, graduation, and early summer, following us like an angel of ironic mercy all the way down to Hatteras for our August vacation.

Nancy's day of deliverance from "the old life" was scheduled for August 14. Hugs and kisses and tears behind us, she and I waved good-bye to the smiling family up on the deck and drove five hours to the university in Chapel Hill. It was, as you might imagine, a bittersweet drive for me. I unloaded the one-ton trunk, four oversize suitcases, and sixteen assorted boxes; got her set up in her dorm; ran errands at the local mall while she attended orientation; had a tender, unsettling last meal at a place called Spanky's on Franklin Street, and headed back to the beach.

The tropical storm Bob I was hearing about on the radio aptly reflected the storm in my heart.

By the time I drove onto the island, Bob was upgraded to a Class 1 hurricane. The following night it was a Class 2. And by the next morning it had made a left sweep, picked up enough steam to be called a Class 3, and was headed toward Hatteras. Two days later we were evacuated.

We didn't want to go home, and motels were booked up a hundred miles in all directions, so we drove to Chapel Hill, rented some hotel rooms, and showed up at Nancy's door at Granville Towers.

Shock, dismay, confusion, nausea, and murderous rage each registered its own particular tic on her pretty face as she stood, speechless, in the doorway.

It was her worst nightmare swirling down the dark tunnel of adolescence. The whole family was following her to college. She would never get away from us, nine of us crowded into a cramped dormitory room barely able to accommodate two.

But like all nightmares, this one came to an end. We stayed a "mere" three days until the evacuation order was rescinded and finally left her alone to live her own life. And she learned her first important college lesson: Thomas Wolfe was wrong—it's not that you can't go home again, you don't ever really leave home at all.

SHE'S LEAVING HOME,
BYE-BYE, PART II

Déjà vu

We die, and we do not die.
    —SHUNRYU SUZUKI

Clover got it exactly right in her "Senior Will" in the yearbook:
"To my older siblings—thanks for molding me so well. To the
young ones—I hope I have done the same for you." The universe is indeed a circle.

From their aggressive style of soccer to their politic manner
as the presidents of SADD (Students Against Drunk Driving) to
the rivalrous ways they preened for the junior prom, Nancy and
Addie preceded and informed Clover about practically everything she would ever experience in high school.

And, like Nancy and Addie when they were seniors, Clover
suddenly couldn't stand being around her home and family.

We were sitting at the dinner table and Danny said something pretty innocuous about a teacher at school and she glared
at him and snapped, "That's not true." Then Patti said something like, "Stacey said that Kitty told her that Dave broke up
with Carrie. . . ."

Fork in midair, sweet, lovable, centered, Zen-like Clover

sneered at her mother like someone from the cast of *90210*: the unbelieving opened mouth, the shake of the head, and then the voice oozing with contempt, "Don't you have a life?"

So when Bay had the audacity to ask her to pass the margarine and when Elizabeth spilled water in her lap, Clover had had enough. She leaped up and scowled, "I can't wait to get out of here!"

We were stunned. Venom like that we could associate with the older crew. Perhaps. But not our sweet little Poochie, who up until that menacing moment had seemed to stroll through life with an aura of quiet at her core.

"Well, before you leave town and change your name," I said, "it's your turn to do the dishes." I thought I was being funny—and it was her turn to do the dishes—but she failed to see the humor in it. She walked out muttering things I'm sure I didn't want to hear. And those of us left behind were once again made to feel like we were residents of a leper colony.

So, there was some cosmic familial justice served up when it came time to grant Clover her wish and take her to college. Ironically, she was following in Nancy's footsteps by going to school in Chapel Hill, and we were again down in Hatteras on vacation, the usual mishmash of kids, dog, parents, boyfriends, girlfriends, coming and going out of the small beach cottage rocking in the wind. And, as it had been laid out four years before, the plan was for me to take Clover over to Chapel Hill midway through the vacation.

It was a beautiful hot day when we first heard about Hurricane Felix being tracked way out in the Atlantic. Clover gasped at the news, but I assured her that lightning doesn't strike the same spot twice.

However, as we tracked the course of the storm from our vulnerable perch on the barrier island, Clover looked on in agitated horror at the unthinkable that seemed to be occurring right before her misting eyes. As if directed by a fate that humbles us all, the hurricane was indeed looping around Bermuda and slowly, surely, almost mindfully, heading for landfall on the Outer Banks.

To Clover's unbelieving dismay, we were evacuated the day before she and I planned to leave.

Poor girl. We packed up the cottage, taped the windows, cleared the decks, and the entire family and the dog drove through wind and rain and flooded roads to take poor old Clover to college. As we trailed her into her dorm room, she looked like she was going to die.

But she didn't.

And along the stormy highway I think Clover learned just what Nancy had learned four years before: you die and you don't die. But you never escape your family.

8

Zen Family Rituals

SEVEN FACTS FOR FATHER'S DAY

Understanding who Father's Day is really for

> *More wisdom is latent in things-as-they-are than in all the words men use.*
>
> —ANTOINE DE SAINT-EXUPÉRY

Into the stupor of half sleep enter footsteps. A covered cough. Something rattling. A whispered *"Hush!"* But the eyelids are heavy. Too heavy. It's Sunday. On Sundays I get to sleep late.

Seconds—or hours—later, with breath sounds close enough to raise the hairs on my neck, I emerge into a dark and dreamy awareness that I am surrounded. Like the child who resides permanently in my soul, I clamp shut my eyes, pretending unconsciousness, hoping the noises and heavy breathing are not from some wild-eyed intruders but from a dream of my own Steven Spielbergian making.

When a sniffling snort pierces the cool morning air, though, one that I instantly recognize as a noise I've heard many times before, and another breathy "Hush!" shakes me to the bone, the synapses click in and I understand in a flash of fear that there are no drug-crazed, knife-wielding criminals in my bedroom. There are no extraterrestrials here. This isn't even a hallucination. Or a nightmare. No, it's something far more frightening ... it's ... it's ...

FATHER'S DAY!!!!!

A silent scream sends me spinning down a circular shaft that I have known only in dreams, but in the moments before I hit bottom (my eyes still closed), I see as clearly as I have ever seen before in my life. Seven facts of life emerge like answers floating to the surface on an old eight ball:

FACT 1: Unless I throw back the quilt and run wailing from the room, I am about to be trapped in an early morning celebration that could rob me of whatever sense of dignity and youth I think I have left. Depending on who's mad at me, who's away at college, and who's still sleeping (when I'm not), from five to seven kids will be grinning as I lift one quivering eyelid to confirm my suspicions. Behind them will stand my oddly smirking wife, Patti, who recently had her own "day," holding a tray of colorfully healthful food I would never consider consuming on an empty stomach.

FACT 2: I can run but I can't hide. They would wake the dog and send her out to track me down. They would demand their due. After all, it's my day and I owe them the once-a-year pleasure of my extreme paternal gratitude and pride.

FACT 3: I will eat ("Mmmmmmmmm") while Elizabeth and Bay mouth along with my every bite; Addie, Nancy, and Cael will twitch impatiently at the edge of the mattress while eyeing the flashing dots on the clock; and Danny and Clover will conspire soundlessly to see who will be the first to jerk my cramped leg, spilling the juice and then the hot coffee in my lap.

FACT 4: Unless I then trade my role as grateful and benevolent papa for the tyrant they always knew I could be, the fruit of my loins will then turn on their heels as if they had actually done their duty and disappear before my rudely awakened eyes. And I'll be left alone to go to the dump, mow the lawn, do some carpooling, and barbecue up a big family dinner that is everyone's vision of a Father's Day repast—except mine. Then I'll open the boxes containing shirts, Day-Glo boxers, and various cassettes and CDs that will be swiped, each by its own giver, by night's end.

FACT 5: (My eyes are still closed.) What I think I'd like is very simple: I'd like to sleep until I can no longer stand to stay in bed. I'd like to take a shower until the hot water starts to run out. I'd like to step into the kitchen to the rousing cheers and tears of a grateful family who would prepare—and leave me alone to eat—some grossly cholesterolic slop. I'd like to read the entire Sunday paper out on the front porch, a cup of chicory coffee at my side and a convenience-store pan of gooey sticky buns right next to it, listening to the dulcet tones of birds, frogs, crickets, and lawn mowers. Next I'd like to get a quilt and lie down on the newly mowed grass so that each of the kids could do twenty minutes massaging my back. Then shoot some hoops. Then a nap. Then a beer, two Nathan's hot dogs with mustard and kraut, followed by some baseball on the tube. Then the big kids would take care of the little kids so Patti and I could escape for a romantic evening at a quaint country inn where we would rediscover what it was that made us want to bring all those children into this world, thus making this day a real celebration.

FACT 6: It (Fact 5) ain't gonna happen. It wouldn't feel like Father's Day to anyone except me, and I might not recognize it at all. (My eyes are *still* closed.) Besides, I came to understand nearly twenty-seven years ago that gratitude is an adult invention. It's not going to happen because my kids take me and their mother and this life for granted.

FACT 7: Kids *should* take their parents for granted. I have never been able to abide trying to make children feel grateful for their very existence. It is I who am grateful every single day for my children, not the other way around.

Children are already painfully aware of their extreme vulnerability in this vast, often cold and perilous world. They need to feel safe, not grateful. It's a parent's job to protect them and build them up, not foster their dependence and fearfulness. As I found out from too many of my teachers back in the fifties and sixties, that fear does not breed gratitude, only contempt. And in answer to those who worry that children who don't learn gratitude at an early age will become self-absorbed adults, I have come to trust that the harsher inevitabilities of life itself will eventually provide enough opportunity for them to learn to be grateful for whatever tasty morsels of goodness come their way. Life happens to all of us.

So I figure that there is no better way to show my gratitude than by allowing my children the pleasure of thinking they are pleasing me on my big day while actually satisfying themselves. As Charles Dickens's forgotten father probably muttered aloud in accepting the toy guillotine young Chucky made him for his birthday, "It is a far, far better thing I do, than I have ever done. . . ."

So I open my eyes, force a goofy smile, and await my fate.

HALF JEW, HALF CHRISTIAN, ALL ZEN

Christmas and Chanukah under one roof

> *Zen is a way of liberation.*
> —ALAN WATTS

I look at my kids—half Jew, half Christian, part believers, part cynics, blue-eyed, brown-eyed, true mongrels in the organized religion sense of the word—and, finally, believe in God. As any father would, I feel my kids are miracles. Each one a blessing.

So I often wonder with profound dismay how any person or any religious group could actually be arrogant enough to believe that one way—their way—is the only pathway to God. All others be damned. How unenlightened.

Frankly, I prefer Gary Snyder's more Zen-like notion that "the way is not a way." That is, there are untold numbers of paths toward the life of pure spirit that awaits each of us. I take comfort in Rabbi Kushner's belief that God grants life but does not inflict injury. God comforts those afflicted with sorrow. And we take care of the rest.

Patti, as true a believer as one may find in an atheist, believes wholeheartedly in the spirit of nature—and celebrates it through the rituals of family dinners, birthdays, and holidays. And although she does a truly admirable job with celebrations like birthdays and Easter and Halloween, December is when she does her finest work. She choreographs, produces, and directs one of the great quasi-religious events in the hemisphere.

Organizationally speaking, Christmas officially begins in our family sometime in July or August when she sees her first "Elizabeth will love this!" doll or some surf shop sweatshirt that she'll buy in sixes for me and all the big kids. By September, with the Christmas club account beginning to flex its muscles, she is already on the lookout for stocking stuffers. And long before the annual New Paltz Halloween Parade, the suddenly closed-to-the-family sewing room will be smothered in boxes, wrapping paper, bows, and presents of every shape, size, weight—and cost.

By the second week in December every surface in the house is decorated. The banister is trimmed with ribbons of pine, the nine stockings hang from the mantel, and the fat tree cut from Van Alst's farm is completely obscured amid the lights, bubblers, and ornaments hauled down in six cartons from the attic.

From there, it's a slippery snowy slope toward the twenty-fifth: baking Christmas cookies, wrapping mountains of presents, singing discordant, repetitive rounds of "The Twelve Days . . ." in the car. College kids (some ours, some not) arrive in the darkest night to change the chemistry of the house.

Then, as if by surprise, it's suddenly Christmas Eve and we're caroling off-key with the Vermilyes at the Coffeys', wrapping more presents, reading "The Night Before Christmas" and St. Luke to everyone in the family, hauling piles of wrapped presents down to the sparkling living room, and then assembling unassembleable toys until two in the morning.

For a Jewish boy it's an annual revelation of joy to watch the seven of them tumble into our bedroom much too early the next morning, each one five years old again and dragging in the loot from an overstuffed stocking, waiting for the word on high that it's time to go downstairs.

*   *   *

In contrast, Chanukah is slightly more low-key.

I prepare for Chanukah by suddenly realizing that the holiday is upon us and I haven't done anything to prepare for it. I scour the cupboards for the menorah and what's left of the candles from previous years, then go to a place like Mr. Jim's Deep Discount and buy odd and sometimes wonderful and always cheap presents for the eight days of the celebration of the miracle of the lights.

Depending on night classes or high school basketball games or Elizabeth's physical therapy or a gazillion other things that get in the way of orderly family life, Chanukah may or may not get going on that first sundown. No big woop.

And given the varying numbers of people who must take part in the ceremonies, and Chanukah's proximity to Christmas, and Addie's birthday (on December 21), and my cosmically disorganized nature, and whether or not I have enough presents if there's an extra boyfriend or two at dinner, the eight-day celebration is often condensed into six or seven or, as happened in 1988, five days covering nearly two and a half weeks. Whatever. It always gets done, and the kids always end up with eight rather odd presents, ranging from temporary tattoos to Rasta necklaces to cassettes and CDs.

The ceremony itself takes less than five minutes. From oldest to youngest, everyone in the family gets a chance to light the candles and say the prayer in Hebrew. Of course, no one knows what it means, but they all like saying the incantation (which they have committed to transliterated near memory) and lighting the candles. Then they all close their eyes and hold out their open palms to receive their earthly goods while I shuffle through the bags of stuff I bought and place one item in each palm. Then I tell them to open their eyes.

And each night they're surprised and a little bit thrilled to get the nonsense I bestow upon them, although more often than not it's left in the dining room, never to be seen again (unless it's still in the package and then I give it to them again the following year).

Although purists would gag at the conceptual Chanukah ceremony that I conduct on (or around) Chanukah each year and others might scorn the lack of subtlety in the Christmas goddess's annual extravaganza, both events have become an enduring part of the way our family lives. In some ways it is an emblem for who we are: Christians, Jews, children liberated from the ridiculous dogma that the unforgiving ascribe to God.

THE LAST ANNUAL NEW YEAR'S EVE PARTY

The times they are a'changin'

> *Don't just do something, sit there.*
> —ANONYMOUS

I can't recall precisely which year it began, the annual New Year's Eve Party for the Homebound and Uninvited, but it was originally devised to save Patti and me and other parents of young children from complete despair on this night of revelry. A noble cause.

New Year's Eve, perhaps the most revered and reviled celebration around North America, is about nothing if not the great second chance. A new beginning. Turning over a new leaf. Redemption. Forgiveness. Pick your banality. Because it has no obvious religious connections, there are no sense of atonement, no apologies, no judgment, no fear; there is only the great relief that one year has passed and a brand-spanking-new one is about to flip up like numbers on digital clocks.

The problem for parents of young children who desperately want to toss away the diaper bag and celebrate a new beginning of civility for just one night is finding a baby-sitter. The entire list of potential sitters scribbled on crumpled sheets of lined paper in the messy kitchen drawer is worthless; they've all got plans.

So, two or three kids into the tribe we call our family, Patti and I were looking ahead to another thrilling New Year's Eve alone with the kids pretending we were having a great time: "It's so much better than all that noise and expense of going out—and for what? It's really about nothing. This is much better." Yeah, right.

That's when some friends, who were as forlorn and homebound as we were, suggested that we cohost a party with them and invite everyone we knew and tell them to bring chips and dips and drinks and, of course, their kids if they didn't have sitters. Unfortunately, the friends were then living in trailers and tiny apartments and couldn't possibly host a party, so we opened our doors.

The house was packed. We ate, we drank, we sang, we danced with babies in our arms, we played puzzles with three-year-olds, we changed diapers, we cleared the linoleum floor and had a dance contest in the kitchen, we crowded into the living room and watched the ball drop in Times Square, we kissed our spouses and kids and other people's spouses and kids, grateful to be out and alive, certain the next year would be easier if not better than the one we'd just survived. At the end of the night the diaper pail was as full as the garbage can.

From there the tradition took on a life of its own. Everyone simply assumed that the Lewises would have the New Year's Eve party. If you didn't have any other place to go—and didn't mind sharing your good time with hippie children who had been taught to be seen and heard—you could always find a party and a dance contest on Coffey Lane. And you could bring your forlorn friends or relatives. Everyone was welcome.

Several years later when Patti and I decided that we definitely didn't want—couldn't afford—definitely would not have— a party, we soon found that the event was totally out of our control. People who we hardly knew would come up to us anytime after Thanksgiving and say, "We'll see you New Year's Eve!"

Anyway, it didn't work. Everyone said New Year's Eve was awful without everyone getting together (at our house), and we should never let it happen again.

And so the party went on like that for years. Then, suddenly(?), the original group of kids grew up and went to their own parties, and their parents, who didn't keep having babies like some people I know, discovered adult, sophisticated New Year's Eves and promptly forgot how much fun we all used to have. And as organically as the party began, it ceased to exist.

The relief was enormous enough to offset any nostalgic notions I might have harbored. The relief was also rather short-lived. Cael, Nancy, and Addie also remembered the wonderful New Year's Eve parties we used to have when they were young and wanted to know what had happened to them. I shrugged, full of hope that their memories were as short as their attention spans.

Yet, as I didn't want them driving on New Year's Eve, I suggested that they invite a few friends over for a "get-together." I didn't want to call it a party, but since we had to chaperon, we invited a few friends over who didn't want to do the typical restaurant–party hopping scene. And the party got a second wind and took on its own momentum.

And sort of left us behind. The first year or two, it seemed to be our affair, with various small pockets of kids sorted by age throughout the house. But then Cael and Nancy were both in college—and Addie and her friends might as well have been— and they were all in the living room, stereo blasting as our rapidly aging friends hid in small pockets in the dining room and kitchen, wishing for earmuffs and waiting uncomfortably until the ball would drop so they could fake some yawns and get the hell out of there.

The passing of one more year brought with it the coup de grâce for the annual fete: hordes of fifteen-year-olds in the basement; throngs of seventeen-year-olds in the attic; twenty-somethings swarming all over the first floor and porches; two nine-year-olds and a six-year-old feigning sleep on the second floor; Hootie and the Blowfish blowing out the woofers on the CD player; televisions flickering all over the house.

And where were Patti and I? Alone, pressed into the far corner of the living room, deserted by the few friends who had come and left before midnight, drinks in hand, speaking fearfully about the cleanup that awaited us and wondering if any of the hordes were going to leave before the bowl games were over the next day.

That was when we decided the tradition was over. *Fini.* As Lou Reed so delicately put it, "Stick a fork in its ass and turn it over, it's done." (However, if our resolve isn't quite what I think it is, and you don't have a sitter, just drop on by. I'm sure we'll be there.)

HERE ONE SECOND, GONE THE NEXT

The importance of family dinners

> *The ritualistic style of conducting one's everyday activities is therefore a celebration of the fact that the ordinary man is a Buddha.*
>
> —ALAN WATTS

Back when Clover was seven or eight, she had a most intriguing quality of falling off her chair at dinnertime. One second she'd be right there alongside six or more other bobbing heads, moving mouths, arms and hands spearing broccoli stalks and shoveling mashed potatoes, and the next second there would be a large gap, like a missing tooth, between Nancy and Danny.

Sometimes you could see it happening in slo-mo: Clover slipping ever so gradually down in her chair until her little chin was just at table level and then—*whoosh!*—she'd disappear as if she'd gone down a flume. Or she'd be listing like the Leaning Tower of Pisa—or a ship about to capsize—and then suddenly roll over and sink in the Bermuda Triangle between the wooden chairs.

However, most of the time our little Clover disappeared from dinner without a conscious notice from anyone, just a sixth sense afterward that something was missing, one of us looking around quizzically and wondering, "Hey, where's Poochie?"

And then Poochie would emerge like a Loch Ness cartoon figure from underneath the table with a goofy embarrassed grin squiggled across her beautiful face. No doubt she had hoped to return to her seat as quietly as she had left it to avoid the shaking heads and the delicious jiggling that comes with swallowing laughter, bursting eyeballs, food running out of Addie's nose.

And thus she came to be called Clummo by her remarkably sensitive brothers and sisters.

But that isn't what this anecdote is really about. Nor is it about the way that Patti and I totally missed another child's medical condition (à la finding out that Danny was practically blind when he went for his kindergarten screening—we thought he fell a lot because he was clumsy). Clover did not fall out of chairs because of some neurological impairment or some middle ear problem that disrupted her balance.

She fell because, as one of the quieter members of the household, she would sometimes zone out on all the bantering and conversation flying around her, facts and falsehoods and accusations crisscrossing the table like the illustrations of airline routes across the country. Stand outside of it for a while, and it's enough to make you dizzy.

I bring it up now because it was Poochie falling out of her chair who came to mind as a metaphor while I was driving away from State College, Pennsylvania, tears slipping from my cheeks every few seconds after dropping off Addie for her freshman year at Penn State.

I simply could not believe that my "pal" had been born and had raced through her childhood before I had time to catch my breath. She was there one day, a twelve-year-old with a ponytail and a turned up nose, and then she was suddenly all grown up and hugging me good-bye. Just like that. Here one second and gone the next.

Just the way Clover used to fall out of her chair at dinnertime. And driving down Route 322 I laughed—and I cried—and I remembered a thousand and one other wonderfully insignificant meals along the parental roadway that I may or may not have eaten alongside my children—and, honestly, may not have really ever occurred as I remember them. But by the time I was nearing Harrisburg, I could taste the eternally sweet longing and the unquenchably bitter remorse that every father knows in his soul; and it was on that ride back to Patti and the kids still at home that I came to know the utter importance of sitting down to eat as a family.

In contrast to whatever some history professor was predictably going to say to Addie about great events that shape our lives—or the individuals who shape great events—I'm certain that it is only the insignificant, ordinary, seemingly forgettable moments that really count in our lives, and few count as resonantly as the ones at meals.

It is there, around the dinner table, that the daily drama gets its dialogue. It is there where we rub shoulders, tell jokes, make gossip, fight, and sometimes even tell of our days; it is there where we brag about our triumphs, where the emptiness of failure or unrequited love finds a loving, if temporary, nourishment that takes you into and through the next day.

In fact, it is right there, between the bread and the butter, where all the great events in life occur; where we make stupid faces at each other and change the course of history; where we catch the sparkling eye of someone who loves us not for what we do or even who we are, but only because we're there, like we're there every day, because we belong there and nowhere else. As Raymond Chandler wrote about breaking bread, it is "a small, good thing." What else is there?

You almost never hear anyone at death's gate regretting that he or she didn't make more money or work longer hours or kill more enemies or write more books or sleep with more people. None of those things really matter. We regret only the life we didn't lead, the insignificant moments lost in chasing after an immortality that was always ours anyway.

At a time when it seems that fewer and fewer families are not only staying together but eating together, the world grows colder and more lonely with each passing meal. Each of us could do much worse than to sit down and eat with the whole family tonight. (If it hurts too much, take a Rolaids.)

DE FACTO ZEN
PARTY FAVORS

Celebrating the eternal inner child

> *How old would you be if you didn't know how old you was?*
>
> —SATCHELL PAIGE

Ten sets of Little Mermaid paper plates and cups are placed around the big pine table. Behind each plate is a formless collection of Starbursts, M&Ms, blowpops, skinny balloons, blow-up gunk, and a party favor chosen specifically for each of the ten party goers. On the bay window is an impressive stack of presents wrapped in Tweety and Sylvester paper, large rectangular clothing boxes and maybe some books and what might be cassettes and perhaps some toys that are packaged in irregularly shaped wrappings.

On the butcher-block kitchen counter is a lopsided, almost beautiful, homemade chocolate sheet cake decorated with blue and pink flowers and squiggles and thin yellow candles. And on the sideboard is the automatic camera loaded with thirty-six-exposure color print film.

Everything is perfect. Picture perfect.

No doubt you're thinking it's Elizabeth's seventh birthday party. It's not. It's Addie's. She's twenty.

Everyone gets the same family party in our house: theme plates, lots of candy, party favors, a homemade cake, and too many presents. Cael's twenty-sixth birthday this summer was, at least before the presents were unwrapped, no different than Bay's ninth or Danny's sixteenth. And they're all caught on film.

As the dad, I am the official photographer for family events. (That's why you rarely see me in family photographs.) I look through the viewfinder, scope out the heartwarming vision, press the button and the light flashes, the camera motor buzzes. Bay, Danny, Addie, and Addie's boyfriend, Nate, are captured forever in their birthday smiles.

Thirty-five pictures left.

Next is the other side of the table: Clover's boyfriend, Jeffrey, Clover, Nancy, Patti, Elizabeth Bayou-Grace. Flash-buzz. Nancy's boyfriend, Michael, walks smilingly into the kitchen, late from work. He's got a present in his hand. Flash-buzz.

There's one of Nate blowing up the gunk. Another of Addie scowling at Jeffrey. Danny bored. Elizabeth giggling. Nancy and Mike kissing. Flash-buzz. The phone rings. It's Cael calling from North Carolina to speak to the birthday girl. Flash-buzz.

The cake. Flash-buzz.

The birthday girl's mother. Flash-buzz.

The birthday girl's mother lighting the candles, walking through the dim room toward the table, placing the shimmering cake in front of the birthday girl. Flash-buzz. She's making a wish, blowing out the candles, cutting the cake, flash-buzz. She's twenty, but behind the sophisticated, faux-embarrassed veneer, there's a six-year-old filled with joy that everybody's there and looking at her and, best of all, bearing gifts. Flash-buzz. Flash-buzz. Flash-buzz.

Patti, the architect of these juvenile celebrations, says everyone's a little kid on their birthdays. Every single one of us not only deserves a *real* party—not some low-key, boring, adult affair at the local chichi restaurant—but in our heart of hearts we all want one with candy and presents and a gooey cake and, of course, party favors. It's virtually impossible to argue with her de facto logic. Just look at the pictures.

Three days later I'll pick up the photos, look at them with a dopey smile before I even leave the camera shop, wondering as I always wonder why I am not in the stack, and look at them again in the car, and look at them again over Patti's shoulder when I get home, providing annoying color commentary all along the way, picture after picture.

Six months later, however, I won't be able to tell you with absolute assurance which number birthday they reflect. All birthdays tend to look alike in four-by-six color, though despite the smug little five-year-old smile on Addie's face when she opened the gold earrings *(Real jew-ler-ee!)*, you can easily identify her as somewhere in college—or, as most people might think, too old to be eating off of Tweety and Sylvester plates and playing with smelly Tubes of Balloons.

Patti would say they don't understand the boundaries of reality.

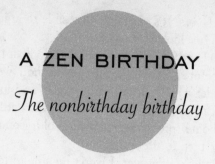

A ZEN BIRTHDAY

The nonbirthday birthday

Sacred cows make great hamburgers.
—ROBERT REISNER

Nancy's old friend and classmate, Whitney, who later became Addie's "squeeze" in high school, a most compelling man-boy who spent an inordinate amount of time in my house playing in the basement with Danny and Bay while he was supposed to be visiting my daughter, taught me about the nonbirthday birthday, or more appropriately, the Zen koan that a truly enlightened individual may indeed have his cake and eat it, too.

I was commandeering a vanload of high school kids to Charlottesville to tour the University of Virginia. I loved—and continue to love—those college trips; out on the open road, tapes blasting, living in motels, walking around all those beautiful campuses, and hanging around with sly, funny, quirky seventeen-year-olds who enable you to remember firsthand how ridiculous adult notions appear to adolescents.

We sat in the rotunda, did the formal tour around Mr. Jefferson's Academical Village, rubbed our hands along the serpentine walls, strolled the charming neighborhood, bought the obligatory UVA T-shirts—and ended up in some college eatery, where the waiters and waitresses had a song-and-dance routine for patrons who were celebrating birthdays. We watched, half amused and half appalled, as the waitstaff burst through the swinging doors of the kitchen doing a kind of bunny hop behind the leader holding the birthday cake and singing a Blue Ridge version of the Beatles' "You say it's your birthday."

We watched as they moved closer and closer to the targeted table, put the cake in front of the surprised and embarrassed and sometimes anguished birthday boy or girl, and then led the entire restaurant in a raucous round of "Happy Birthday to You." Very funny. Pretty awful.

Anyway, we ate, laughed at the birthday train, which reappeared three more times, ate some more, talked college admissions, gossiped, goofed on our fellow diners, and generally acted our age—except, of course, me. And that was it.

Just about the time that I started looking for our waiter to ask for the check, though, the conga line burst into the dining room again, holding a cake and singing, "They say it's your birthday. . . ." We groaned; we laughed; we watched as the line snaked its way around the restaurant, wondering who was the next poor soul to be embarrassed. And I slouched back in my chair, just plain annoyed because I wanted to get on the road and I knew we wouldn't get the check until after the ceremony was over.

The singers danced their way between the tables, seeming to stop for a moment only to tease the crowd and bunny hop along once again, heading toward our side of the room.

I glanced over at the tables on either side of us trying to figure out who was "it," and by the time I looked up again it actually seemed as if they were coming right at us like some calypso-driven tornado, surrounding our table and dropping the cake right down in front of me, *me!* Everyone laughing and singing, all those teeth smiling, fingers pointing, and Whitney Smith suddenly leaping up and yelling, "Happy Birthday Dad, you're the greatest!"

Everyone in the restaurant cheered and sang the song and howled as I turned deep crimson and fought the urge to crawl under the table and bite off Whitney's leg at the knee.

Of course, I didn't tell my fellow revelers that my birthday is not October 22nd, it's April 30th; nor that Whitney is not my son but was spending so much time at my house I was thinking of listing him as a dependent; nor even that I respected the transcendent manner in which Whitney had figured out a way to have his cake and eat it, too.

And then have someone else pay for it.

THE ANNUAL EASTER EGG HUNT

Addie's boyfriend, Nate, a dental student, joins the first and third graders for the annual Easter egg hunt in our backyard

In zazen, one is one's present self, what one was, and what one will be, all at once.

—PETER MATTHIESEN

One of the more remarkable clichés that gets coughed up whenever people find out that I have seven kids is "They must keep you young."

I figure that anyone who would say something like that must be temporarily blinded by the concept of having more children than you can count on one hand. I mean, just look at me: the wild gray hair, the manifest destiny bald spot encroaching on my forehead, the lines around my deep-set eyes that suggest one too many nights spent waiting up for teenagers to get home.

Young seems a rather limited view of my present circumstances.

I'm more inclined to see my age in terms of Matthiesen's vision of zazen, all things at once. There are moments in the midst of every day when I feel so worn out by living my life in nine places at one time that I feel older than my octogenarian parents. But a few minutes later I'm two again and I don't wanna share my tools (clothes, car, food, etc., etc., etc.) with anyone. *Anyone!*

Sometimes, when I'm having a tea party with Elizabeth, I have the extraordinary sensation of being six and sixty-six at the same time. Other times, when I'm just hanging out in the kitchen with Danny or Clover and yammerin' about concerts and movies and who's doin' what to whom, I feel eighteen again, ready to party my semiconscious way through weekend nights at Wheatley High. And when I'm having a catch with Bay, I might as well be nine once more, dripping with laughter and mud, imagining myself climbing the center field wall of Ebbets Field like Duke Snider about to rob the Say Hey Kid of another home run.

Last year's Easter egg hunt provided a particularly instructive manifestation of Mathiessen's principle. On Patti's instructions, the little kids were sent to the basement while the older kids and visiting parents, acting as crew members for her annual spectacular, were out in the yard hiding dyed eggs and chocolate kisses and all the other delicious substances banned by the American Dental Association on tree limbs, behind rocks, in the mesh of the hammock—anywhere out of reach of the sniffing nose of the chocoholic dog.

Then Patti called down to the kids, maybe twenty of them, to come up on the back deck and receive their final instructions for Operation Easter: first graders anywhere in the yard; third graders must search beyond the swing set; fifth graders and all others will confine their hunt to the front yard, the stream, and the woods.

Standing behind and above the hordes on the deck was Nate, Addie's boyfriend: twenty-two years old, six feet four inches tall, about to graduate from Cornell University and go off to dental school. At first I thought he was helping Addie organize the little guys, but then I noticed the same gloriously expectant look in his eyes that lit up the faces of six-year-old Zoe and ten-year-old Craig—not to mention the pink and yellow and blue basket he was carrying. And when he yelled out, "Where do the sixteenth graders go?" I knew that he had transcended time and space and entered Mathiessen's realm.

Like a giraffe among dwarf chimpanzees, Nate raced off the

deck with the rest of the kids when Patti gave the signal to go searching for goodies left by the Easter Bunny. Then I noticed tenth grader Danny and twelfth graders Clover and Jeffrey following close behind Nate with baskets in their hands. (Several minutes later Patti caught them exchanging "good" candy they were just finding with "bad" candy they had already found.)

They weren't the only adult-size children, though. I saw Kathleen's grandmother snarf a marshmallow bunny when she thought no one was looking; I saw IBM manager Joe Ferri stuffing his mouth with the sweets he was supposed to be hiding for the children, looking remarkably like his own six-year-old, Dara. I was even nabbed: Elizabeth wanted to know how I got all that chocolate smeared on my face.

She's too young to know that all things happen at once. I told her that her mother kissed me.

9

Zen Vacations on the Road of Life

OUTER BANKS AT NIGHT

What you see is never what you get

If you meet the Buddha on the road, kill him!
—ZEN SAYING

A popular postcard found in many resort areas is all black. Actually, it's glossy black and on the bottom in small white type it reads "Outer Banks (or Big Sur or Cape Cod or . . .) at Night."

Many people who see it for the first time while spinning the postcard rack at the local surf shop smile and pluck it out to show to someone else. Then the two of them laugh a little conspiratorially. It's funny. And stupid.

But it's also kind of wry, a subtle swipe at the amount of time, energy, and money spent on gathering artificial evidence in the form of snapshots of the ahness of travel. And perhaps even more remarkable is the fact that most people get the joke, five-year-olds as well as seventy-five-year-olds. It is a perfect representation of the Zen of family vacations. The beautiful postcard—as the beautiful photograph—is everything travel is and also everything travel is not.

All of us in our hearts understand the patent phoniness of the photographic image. The blue sky is often softer and bluer than it really was. In the foamy surf you can't see the perilous undertow. There's no accounting in the flat image for the heat or the humidity or the mosquitoes in the air. The smiles on the tanned faces of the family suggesting pure harmony often cover the angst of ongoing family skirmishes. And you never hear dad behind the viewfinder, yelling, "Smile, dammit!"

My most successful vacation in terms of Zen photography came in 1986. The proof comes by way of the fact that I don't actually have the snapshots in hand. Or in an album. Yet I'm sure the pictures were perfect. They were perfect because I know I had what might best be termed a lapse of consciousness and, in effect, pressed down a little too hard on the shutter and captured the essence of vacations in a single moment.

Several of the kids and I were at Island Convenience, a Texaco station, tackle shop, grocery store, snack shop, and souvenir stand run by Mac and Marilyn Midgett, and I was suddenly inspired to take the annual "child pumping gas" shot. It was the last shot on the roll, the camera automatically whirring its way through the rewind. And then just as suddenly the automatic shut-off on the gas gun clicked.

I put the camera on the rear bumper of the van, took the hose from whichever child was with me, and dribbled in a few more drops of gas, replaced the cap, and walked my barefoot way into the cool store. While on line I picked up some candy, made some weather talk with a fisherman, paid the damage, walked out into the blazing sun, and hoisted myself back into the driver's seat. I shared whatever candy I didn't hide for myself alone. I turned the ignition. I clutched, jammed the shift into reverse (a car was in front of me), turned myself all around so I could be absolutely sure I wouldn't hit anyone or anything, and backed up maybe a yard or two until I heard a crack and a crunch and some kind of minor implosion.

I knew immediately what it was. (You don't have to run this father over with the facts.) And what it was not.

Upon reflection, I'm certain that roll contained more beautiful photographs than I had ever taken before or have taken since. Being lost in the nothingness of the twisted metal and splintered plastic and ripped celluloid under my F75-14 rear tires, they remain a perfect vision of what a beach should forever be: the family vacation at total eclipse.

THE INEFFABILITY OF
FAMILY VACATIONS

The pain of pleasure

> *The only Zen you find on the tops of mountains is the Zen you bring up there.*
>
> —ROBERT PIRSIG

As an unbroken survivor of all-night drives to the Outer Banks of North Carolina in a VW van with seven kids (a dog, a roof rack, a turtle top, four bikes, a moped, and enough bungee cords to do a successful jump off the George Washington Bridge) as well as camping washouts in Martha's Vineyard, a car fire in Delaware, brake failure in Virginia, botched reservations in Florida, barfing children in Jersey, three hurricanes on Hatteras, a midnight call from a constable in London, roseola in the Hamptons, fever hallucinations in Naples, island hopping in Hawaii, missed planes, lost directions, lost wallets, lost kids, lost patience, lost nerve, and lost expectations, I am intimately aware of the darker pitfalls of family vacations.

Yet there is nothing I yearn to do more than hoist my dadself into the Vanagon and travel off to the next adventure with my wife and kids.

Viewed from a detached perspective, vacations for fathers represent Zen in its purest form: the agony of pleasure. Most of us spend the entire year (minus two days)—no exaggeration—looking forward to lying back and enjoying some pure unfettered time with the family. No work, no boss, no shoes, no underwear, no shaving, just flyin' kites and buildin' sand castles and fishin' with the kids—and at night renewing the steamy love affair with the woman who inspired the desire to fly kites and build sand castles and fish with those kids.

The oddly wonderful thing about *male vacation envy* is that it's built solely on a mushy foundation of the American Family Togetherness Myth and tempered by the cartoonish stresses brought on by TV family life and hardened into plasticene reality by much-smaller-than-life advertisements for "Family Fun Getaways."

From the day after a man returns from vacation and goes back to work (and has miraculously forgotten the undifferentiated anxiety he experienced less than forty-eight hours before) to the morning nearly a year later that he must pack up the car with enough equipment and clothing to outfit a third-world nation, he believes in his heart that he really wants to go on vacation again.

It's quite sublime, the way the grass keeps growing. And the perennial beauty of it is that as the weeks and months pass by, dads are made increasingly happy by increasingly faulty memories of the previous year's litany of disasters. Desiring nothing more than to get away from it all—and seduced by the patently ridiculous notion that a bad day of fishing (surfing, hunting, bird watching, yadda yadda yadda) is better than a good day at work—dads all over must annually relearn the three universal unkind truths of family travel:

1. Daily life goes on. You don't leave it behind. Kids fight with each other, whine, wake up too early or too late, get sick, get bored, get lost, get your goat, and spend all your money.
2. It takes only twenty-seven minutes to spend all the money you made in fifty-four hours the week before you left on vacation.
3. Family restaurants suck.

THE SPIRIT OF A MEXICAN VACATION

The revenge of Montezuma

> *He who knows does not speak;*
> *He who speaks does not know.*
> —LAO-TZU

When the advance-grant (for a textbook I was writing) arrived, we should have promptly put the money in the bank, but it was such a nice even figure and I had a February vacation coming up, and the family tour package to Cancún sounded cheaper than staying home, *and* it seemed like a once-in-a-lifetime cultural experience for the kids. Besides, it was minus twenty degrees in New Paltz.

Plans were hastily made, reservations confirmed, and even though I received a speeding ticket en route to Kennedy Airport, everything couldn't have been more perfect. The nine of us (five kids, two parents, two grandparents) arrived in Cancún and were transported to one of the glitzy hotels along the strip. It didn't look much like Mexico—more like a fancy Miami Beach—but the local people looked Mexican and spoke Spanish and, hey, the water was as blue as in the brochures.

The first problem I encountered involved the difficulty in understanding the clerk behind the reservations desk. The second was revealed when I finally understood why he wasn't giving me the keys to our rooms: the hotel was overbooked.

While Patti opened the suitcases, found bathing suits, and undressed and dressed the little kids in the middle of the lobby (while the older kids hid behind the potted palms in mortal embarrassment), I had an all-American tantrum. I yelled, I cursed, I pleaded, I threatened lawsuits, I tried bribery. All to no avail. *No comprendo, Señor.*

I called the inept travel agent back home, who didn't know what he could do for us "all the way down there." I called the tour company, which wouldn't be open until Monday morning at nine o'clock. I even tried phoning the U.S. Consulate, but no one answered.

I also called every hotel on the beach in Cancún, but they were all overbooked. Late that afternoon, tired of my yelling and afraid that we'd never leave the lobby, the hotel management offered to put us up in the center of Cancún for the night. We had no choice. Suffice it to say that because the replacement hotel was right in the middle of a filthy and vermin-infested neighborhood, it also lacked the gorgeous white sand beach. However, we did find some unlabeled pharmaceuticals in the bathroom and a pair of stiff men's underpants underneath the bed. I stayed up all night guarding my family from bad hombres with crisscrossed gun belts and in the morning called every hotel on the Yucatán Peninsula trying to salvage the already decimated vacation.

In retrospect, I guess I should have known that something was wrong when I found the only hotel in the region with vacancies. But a few hours later we were on the exotic isle of Cozumel, and the hotel lobby didn't look so bad at all and the extraordinarily blue Caribbean was even more beautiful than in Cancún, and even if there was a disconcerting smell as we entered the lobby and the rooms were a little mildewy, I just knew it was going to be wonderful. This was the real Mexico, not some Epcot version of foreign lands. Now the kids would really have a cultural experience.

And they certainly did. We snorkeled all afternoon, spoke halting Spanish to the natives, ate a real Mexican dinner (being very careful not to drink the water or eat fresh fruit and vegetables), walked around the beautiful square in San Miguel, and went to sleep full of the spirit of Central America.

Clover, who was in the room with Patti, Danny, and me, was the first to lose that spirit. In the hopes of keeping this on a higher plane, let's just say that she lost her spirit a few steps before reaching the bathroom. And moments later she was overcome with an almost uncontrollable urge to lose the spirit from a different, deeper, and darker, aspect of her being.

Then, as I was helping poor Clover in the bathroom and Patti was tending to the loss of spirit on the rug, Patti up and lost her spirit. A minute later I lost mine. Shortly thereafter, Clover lost hers once more—in the bed this time. Then Patti. Then me.

And just about the time that we thought the great spirit festival was complete, Montezuma began his rumbling deep in the parental maw. First me, then Patti racing to the porcelain altar like a woman who'd seen the Mayan devil.

Meanwhile, five-year-old Danny, who we affectionately called Dirty Dan because of his abhorrence of the tools of normal hygiene, slumbered as calm and unfettered as if he were cradled in the bosom of the gods.

Practically spiritless by then, I garnered enough energy to put on some clothes and go next door to see how Cael, Nancy, and Addie were faring. When I opened the door, Addie looked absolutely fine, but Cael was already light green and moaning on the bed, alternately threatening and begging Nancy to get out of the bathroom where she'd apparently been meditating on her own spirit loss for the last fifteen minutes.

It was only then, I must add, that things really got nasty.

With no notice and no explanation—*No hablo inglés, Señor*— the management suddenly turned off the water in the hotel! Wide-open taps; unflushable toilets; the transmogrifying aroma of earthly spirit permeating the air.

I won't go into detail about how we had run out of towels and were using sheets and yesterday's shirts to clean up after ourselves, but the final transcendent moment came several minutes later when Addie pushed open our door, took one look around at the devastation, mumbled something about "not feeling so good anymore," and unleashed a projectile offering to the gods that landed all over the curtains.

And Danny continued to sleep through it all.

I eventually made it out to a bodega and bought six bottles of the pink stuff, slugged one down like it was a cool Corona, and returned to administer the nectar to my dis-spirited family. And that afternoon, after the water was turned back on and all of us felt barely well enough to sit on the gorgeous white beach, we watched Danny frolic alone in the surf.

It turned out, as you home repair dads may have already surmised, that the hotel had a problem with sewage leaching into the water supply. In the end, it didn't matter that no one in the family drank the water. And no one ate raw fruit or vegetables. No one even slipped and ordered ice for the drinks. But we did brush our teeth.

Everyone got sick. Everyone, that is, except five-year-old Dirty Dan, who in those days would do anything to avoid bathing or even brushing his teeth. He played all afternoon on the coral reef and ate another big dinner that night—and found in Mexico the perfect place to maintain his spirit through cultural enhancement.

BEING THERE—AND NOT BEING THERE

A trip to the Magic Kingdom

When you put Bay to sleep at night, he boards a space vehicle for transport to his home planet.
—RICHARD GAYNOR, ZEN MASTER

As every parent knows, children are transcendent beings. They are not limited by the five senses or conventional notions of what-you-see-is-what-you-get reality. They are larger than life. And much, much smaller.

In fact, they are pure spirit, like angels. They have (so-called) imaginary friends; they talk to trees, animals, inanimate objects; they make observations about the world that are so nonsensical that wizened adults are suddenly able to see life in an entirely new dimension. In short, they have extraordinary powers of imagination and perception that enable them to envision fantastic visions as true reality.

On a family vacation that could be a real problem.

I'm sure you've noticed—or remember the sensation from your own unforgotten childhoods—that no matter where you take children for the first time, no matter how excited they are to be going there, or how many times they have to pee before they get there, or how often you must yell at them to stop jumping up and down and shrieking in delirium in the backseat of the family van as you approach the palace of their dreams, there is always a profound sense of disappointment in their eyes or the lilt of their voices as soon as you finally get there. Wherever. The circus. Hawaii. Yankee Stadium. The New York City Ballet. Walt Disney World. Wherever. As Peggy Lee sang years ago, "Is that all there is?"

It's a terrible—and indeed terrifying—moment of existential awareness for parents. Yet we have so much invested in our children's happiness, and harbor such tender hidden memories of our own similarly profound disappointments as children, that we constantly strive to bring the light of pure joy into our children's eyes.

Why else would anyone take their children to Walt Disney World?

When Patti and I announced at dinner that we were thinking of taking the family to the Magic Kingdom, it was as if a marching band stepped out of the wallpaper and strobe lights appeared on the ceiling and thousands of little children started laughing and applauding us—the most wonderful parents on the face of the earth.

Thus deified, we flew to Tallahassee to visit Cael at college and then motored down to Orlando, the electricity in the backseats making the rental van glow and shimmer as we hovered above I-75 and passed through Kissimmee, where it seems there are more billboards than people.

We parked in the Goofy parking lot, took the Little Train That Could to the monorail that whisked us silently into the dimension of transcendent fun, and then racewalked through the gates of the Magic Kingdom. Wide-eyed and white-knuckled, the children paused briefly to soak in the magic that appeared before their unbelieving eyes.

Which is when I saw the archetypal flash of disappointment skitter across the smooth faces of the older children. If their expressions were translatable, they would probably have read, *This is incredible, but it's just a big, fancy amusement park. It's not beyond my wildest expectations.*

But not Bay. Opaquely self-centered and translucently selfless, he is the one child among our seven who is seemingly the least entangled by damning realities. Exuberance resonates in all that he does. He is a gift from the cosmos to open up the doors of perception.

So while his siblings paused briefly to acclimate themselves to the less-than-magic reality, Bay was running around in circles screaming that he could see Mickey and Donald and Dumbo—and following his spirited lead, everyone released the tenacious grip on their varied disappointments and had a wonderful time, boarding every ride in the park, buying ridiculous souvenirs, and eating enough hot dogs, french fries, fried dough, Cokes, candy, and ice cream to feed any one of the Epcot-centered nations.

When it was finally time to go back to the motel, we had spent all our money, all our energy, all our good sense—and all our collective disappointment.

I was completely and utterly depleted. I followed Patti and the kids onto the Little Train That Could, happy for the good day we'd had, hopeful that I might never have to have another good day like that again. As we drove slowly back through the Goofy parking lot, I closed my eyes and leaned back in the seat thinking of nothing but the bed in the motel room.

That's when Bay yanked on my shirt and said, "So, Daddy, when are we going to Dismey Whirl?"

My mouth dropped open. "What?"

"When are we going to Dismey Whirl?" Several hundreds of dollars, eight stained shirts, and some serious indigestion after a full day at the Magic Kingdom, and Bay wanted to know when we'd be going to *the* Disney World.

The doors of perception opened a little wider for me at that moment. Bay may have only been three years old then, but he knew that the big smelly mouse wasn't Mickey, that the ridiculous felt duck wasn't Donald, and that Space Mountain didn't really take you into space. Of course.

He'd had a great time, but now he wanted to go to the real thing, the *real* Magic Kingdom.

We couldn't fool him. Walt Disney couldn't fool him.

What could I say? I closed my eyes again and told him what parents all over the solar system tell their kids: we'd get there . . . sometime.

THE ROAD OF LIFE

*How a nine-hour Sunday drive turns into
a thirteen-hour marathon tour of pitstops*

*Flow with whatever may happen and let your mind be
free: Stay centered by accepting whatever you are doing.
This is the ultimate.*

—CHUANG-TZU

Paul Ruff, the Mario Andretti of the family station wagon, makes the 540-mile drive to Hatteras Island from upstate New York in around nine hours. I marvel at his paternal control, his capacity to maintain focus in a steel cage full of children, his ability to hurtle through space at speeds just below radar detection. More than a man's man, he is a father's kind of father.

As I've heard it described, Paul packs the family (four kids, a friend or two, and his wife, Lynn) into the Chevy wagon, positions himself in the cockpit, locks the doors, turns up the AC, and leadfoots his way for three hundred miles or so deep into Delaware, where he stops just long enough for everyone to rush to the bathrooms, grab a snack, and race back to the car before the gas nozzle clicks off—and then he locks the doors again and barrels down through the Delmarva across the Chesapeake Bay Bridge-Tunnel and along the coast all the way to the Outer Banks. That's it. Nine hours. Holy. Holy. Holy.

In striking contrast is my thirteen-hour stop-and-start tour of natural and man-made pissoirs along the Atlantic seaboard. So, just about the time that the Ruffs would be pulling in to Rodanthe, the Lewis clownmobile is predictably located somewhere around Onancock on the eastern shore of Virginia, chugging its way into the fourth or fifth Texaco station, Patti and the children racing knock-kneed for the bathrooms while I'm checking the ropes and bungees and duct tape holding everything together.

I'm not sure whether it's a case of genetically small bladders or chronic urinary tract infections or just simple lack of good old Presbyterian self-control—or perhaps an overwhelming desire to purge the body of toxins—but my family has a patent inability to drive more than a hundred and nineteen minutes without wetting their pants. (That is, everyone except Nancy and me, who not only share the same birthday but the same constitution, including a gallon-size bladder.)

The rest of the group obviously got Patti's three-teaspoon-size organ. Addie, for example, can't make the four-hour drive to school at Penn State without at least one yellow-eye stop, and Cael can't do the two hundred miles from Durham to Hatteras along Highway 64 without stumbling out beyond the tree line once or twice. Even the simple ninety-mile trip to New York City from our home in the Shawangunk Mountains is often punctuated by at least one rest stop; and if Bay is along for the ride, we may have to stop twice.

The good thing about Bay is that, like most boys, he'll go anywhere—in the bushes, behind a tree, behind a Pizza Hut, in the dunes, off a porch, anywhere. Just as the Jeff Goldblum character says in *The Big Chill*, "That's what I love about the outdoors: it's one big toilet." And so it is for Bay.

Patti, the earth mother, is just like Bay, at least in her willingness to do what comes naturally, naturally. She will drop and squat behind any available tree along the side of practically any road that is not in the Bronx or Brooklyn. Unfortunately, the three older girls in the family consider doing their business along the side of any road an abomination. They would rather turn jaundiced, explode, and die than pee in the woods. They absolutely refuse.

So I stop at the first public restroom on the highway. And 119 minutes later I stop at another. And then another. And another.

But unscheduled restroom stops are not the sole reason why the avatar Paul Ruff beats me to Hatteras by four hours. Five, six, even seven stops along the side of the road to pee would add only an hour or so to the trip. But since we have to find a place with a clean toilet, no less, practically every stop also has a retail purchase element to it, which invariably includes a drink. ("I'm dying of thirst, Dad.")

If I balk at buying drinks, everyone, including Patti, looks at me as if they're one step away from calling 911. And, of course, they don't just buy drinks, they get fries and chips and whatever else is *absolutely* necessary. ("After all, Dad, we're stuck in this van for thirteen hours.") And 119 minutes later we'll have to stop again, where they'll want a whole new round of sodas because all the chips they ate in the intervening two hours made them so thirsty that they'd *die* if they didn't get another drink . . . and so it goes.

Years ago I sopped trying to fight biological and psychic reality. If the trip takes us thirteen hours, then so be it. Crank up Bob Marley or Van Morrison or Lou Reed, get into a travelin' groove, and go with the endless flow of karmic traffic. I might never make it to Hatteras in nine hours, but last year, as we rumbled through Temperanceville, Virginia, my mind flowed so freely that I had a vision of the purity of line, the oneness with the machine, the spiritual connection to the road that Paul Ruff achieves every August: one stop for gas on the way to nirvana. Selah! Selah! Selah!

THE ZEN OF GETTING CLEAN IN RURAL CONNECTICUT

Gender discrimination in a campground shower

God is in the details.
—MIES VAN DER ROHE

Even with charmingly primitive signs nailed to trees and stuck in soft grassy shoulders along the chip and oil roads winding around the gracious Connecticut countryside, we had to retrace our steps several times before arriving at the campground. It should have been as simple as sleeping under the stars: Route 202 to Milton Road to Maple Road to Hemlock Hill Road, but as those of us who have grown middle-aged in the shadows of Ram Dass and Ronald Reagan understand, simplicity is never simple.

The ad in *Woodall's* said we'd find "friendly people, a beautiful setting, and well-maintained modern facilities." And down the long dirt road, that is nearly what we found: friendly people in a nice setting, though a tad swampy down near our campsite.

And that would have been that had I not had this odd misunderstanding about the showers. Not that they weren't reasonably modern and pretty well maintained. But after a restless night punctuated by bullfrogs twanging and a tree root that seemed to follow my every diversionary movement, daybreak filtering into the cold dewy tent along with the voice of someone from a neighboring site calling for my daughter Clover, or, as it turned out, calling for a dog with the same name, I would have settled for a trickling hose. All I wanted was water on my head.

Nancy was the first to make the trek to the facilities but returned shortly with the news that the showers cost a quarter for six minutes. No big deal; we scrounged the floor of the VW bus for coins, and as unspoken family tradition dictated, I waited with the baby and the boys (who never even considered showering) until the women got back.

Finally, it was my turn. Soap, towel, toothbrush, change of clothes, and quarter in hand, I strode into the comfortably campy, lightly mildewed men's room like a gunslinger into a bar. There was a man at one of the sinks shaving all around his pencil-thin mustache. With respect for the ancient ritual, I nodded briefly in the mirror and ducked into the shower stall.

Soon naked, except for my quarter, I looked up. I looked down. I turned around. I turned all the way around again but could not find the coin slot anywhere. One more orbit within the tiny stall and I wrapped the towel around my waist and walked out to the sink area, certain the mechanism must be there. It wasn't.

The shaving man watched me in the mirror as I looked around with a scowl on my face, but he did not say a word. Nor did I, stepping back into the stall and scanning the walls, ceiling, and floor one more time for the slot. It was nowhere.

Of course I felt inept for missing something that should have been so obvious, but as I wrapped the towel around me one more time and stepped out to ask the shaver if he knew where the thing might be, it seemed I had little choice.

He shrugged and said, "I went swimming," as if he owed me an explanation.

I returned his shrug and, with nowhere else to go, walked out into the hall. I'm not sure what I expected to find out there other than a washing machine, a dryer, a bulletin board of local attractions, and a mimeographed list of the day's activities. Two women sorting laundry stopped talking, glared at my towel, and turned away.

Frankly, I was lost. I considered walking back to the campsite to ask my wife or one of my daughters where the mechanism was hidden, but as that would predictably be fraught with laughter and derision, I opted to give the shower one more try. The man arched one eyebrow as I appeared in the frame of the door. I shook my head and disappeared again behind the curtain, dropped the towel, and scanned the white stall. In desperation I decided to simply turn the knobs and see what would happen.

What happened was that the water came on. I nearly shrieked in cold panic, but not being alone, I kept it to myself. I did, however, feel as though I owed the shaver an explanation, so I poked my head around the plastic curtain and called out, "It works! It's free! They must just charge the women"—the absurd reality was just then sinking in, like water swirling down the drain.

He was at the door, turning and smiling like Boston Blackie, the arc of the mustache flattening out across a wide gap-toothed leer. "It's about time we got somethin' for free."

Out of pure orneriness, I took a twenty-minute scalding hot shower and left the water running while I toweled off, dressed, and rehearsed my indignation for the manager.

The camp store was empty, though. At first I considered snagging a few Snickers from a ripped display box as payment for the women's showers but instead picked up a local newspaper off the counter while I waited.

On page three there was a headline from a Gannett News Service story on sex discrimination: STUDY: WOMEN MAKING LITTLE PROGRESS ON PAY SCALE. I nodded. We make them pay every step along the way.

10

More Is Less:
The Zen of Living Large
on a Small Planet

A FATHER'S NUMEROLOGY

Calculating freedom

> *Freedom's just another word for nothing left to lose.*
> —KRIS KRISTOFFERSON

In the weeks following Nancy's birth in 1973, I spent many late nights pacing the living room floor with our beautiful, fat, *howling* baby girl in my weary arms. On one of those long and harrowing sojourns nowhere, I found that I could control my frustration and maintain my sanity by calculating the years that it would take until the collicky baby would grow up—and I would be free again.

I figured that when Nancy reached eighteen—and Cael twenty-two—I would be free. Free, that is, to be me. Me, the well-regarded writer and teacher I knew was my destiny. The day Nancy would leave for college to seek her destiny, I'd set sail on my own journey of self-actualization. I would be forty-five, still young enough to take advantage of the freedoms that would be mine simply by relinquishing my role as worrier and protector—and late-night pacer—a role she would no longer want me to serve. Nancy and I would be friends together in the real world of 1991, not Dada changing a messy diaper, or Daddy booting a soccer ball to his daughter, or even Dad pacing the living room at night waiting for the headlights in the driveway. We would be friends, talking politics or literature or whatever over a beer at Tony's Tavern.

That simple arithmetic helped me get through the colic that evening; and from that vantage point I could foresee a full life ahead to take care of my needs again—to go out when I wanted, to go to exotic places, to sleep late, to sleep long, to be me. Fathering two children, like going to college, was something I did en route to something else. My *real* identity was deeper, more complex than that. It just took some calculations.

And eighteen years later, when I woke up the morning after Nancy's first visit home from college, I remembered those simple calculations and understood with a tired yawn just how wrong they had been. What started out as a small hippie family of four, as you know, blossomed into a not-so-small tribe of seven kids who have defined life and freedom for me in ways I never envisioned on that night in 1973.

Yet all these years have shimmered past like a meteor and I still find myself awake in the middle of the night, up with Elizabeth, who has her own bad dreams, or growling at Bay and his friend Luke to "Go to sleep, now!" or listening almost breathlessly until I hear Danny walk through the front door after curfew.

Through my children's enduring presence, I know myself a little better now than I did when I paced the floor with Nancy all those years ago. I see more clearly my destiny today, even as I am drawn ineffably toward the infinite. When people ask what I do, I still sometimes tell them out of habit or convenience—or some vestige of those days on North Newhall Street—that I am a writer and a teacher, wishing, I think, to add some unnecessary weight to my mere presence. But at the core of my pulsing heart I know I am not a writer or a teacher.

I am a father. I have been a father since I was a few steps out of my father's house. I have been a father for longer than it took John Keats to live a whole life and immortalize himself as a writer.

I am a father when I stand in front of a class, when I sit at a computer screen, coach a Little League team, mow a lawn, plunge a toilet, read a poem, sing a song, sit on a beach . . . as I weep even as I laugh at it all. I will probably be lying awake, pacing the floor, arguing paradoxical points of childhood logic long after I am also a grandfather.

I am a father. That is all I am.

FOOD IS LOVE

The cost of feeding the masses

> *One cannot think well, love well, sleep well, if one has not dined well.*
>
> —VIRGINIA WOOLF

One night this past summer, after a particularly hot and grueling fourteen-hour day of work, I stumbled through the kitchen doorway and headed straight for the fruit bowl.

I yearned only to dump my heavy knapsack, cradle a cool round peach in my palm, walk into the living room, fall back onto the couch, and bite into something that would dribble down my chin and reinvigorate my taste buds and wet my dry throat.

But the wooden fruit bowl on the counter was empty, or practically empty, a few straggly grapeless vines, two wrinkled mangy-looking grapes, some peach stems, and a two-week-old black and purple banana.

I looked forlornly over to Patti, and in my most understanding and deviously needling voice said only, "Didn't make it to the fruit market today?"

"I did!" she snapped, as if she'd seen right through my veneer of sensitivity. But it was just futility speaking. "I spent forty-six dollars and that's what's left, except the damn banana, of course. Why don't they ever eat the last banana?"

I pondered the unponderable. "I don't know." Then I remembered the problem at hand. "How did they eat forty-six dollars' worth of fruit in an afternoon?" I asked incredulously, as if I didn't already know. Patti and I find ourselves often playing the role of the Costello straight man to the other's Abbott when it comes to matters of finance. It's simply amazing to consider how much food can be consumed by a family of nine.

In Patti's tight-lipped response to my incredulity lies the reason: "When I came home they were all sitting around the kitchen counter like vultures, complaining that there was no food in the house. They devoured most of the grapes before I even got them in the bowl."

Craig, Bay's BIG friend, was visiting; and Danny and his pal Keith awakened from their Nintendo-induced stupor in the basement when they sniffed fresh food in the air; and Nate, Michael, and Jeffrey (boyfriends) all showed up just before dinner; and Elizabeth did her usual: she takes a bite of some fruit, puts it down, and promptly forgets about it—and then later gets another piece of fruit and takes a bite out of that one and puts it down. That night I found four pieces of rotting fruit all around the house.

I nodded and tried to figure out how long it takes me to make forty-six dollars, but my brain was too fried. I opened the refrigerator and snatched the one remaining Corona from the six-pack I'd bought the night before, grateful that they had at least left me something cold and wet.

Employing pure logic, you'd think that with Cael grown and moved on, leaving us with eight in the house, we'd consume exactly twice as much as the typical family of four.

Wrong. Food has no logic; consumed exponentially as the numbers around the table increase, Patti says that the cooking itself for eight or nine, which should involve no more work or preparation, is easily more than twice as time-consuming and perhaps three times more costly than feeding a family of four. I know, it doesn't compute.

There are two units of cost factors in any family: consumables and wearables. Wearables, which include shoes, clothes, sports equipment, coats, etc., may be stroke-inducingly expensive, but at least you can cut the cost by shopping for sales and handing things down. Bay, who must have forty T-shirts (no exaggeration), probably has only five that have been exclusively his from point of purchase. Elizabeth is wearing dresses today that were bought in 1973 and worn by all three older sisters. Danny—and the big girls—are continual beneficiaries of the weeding of my closet. Even cars get handed down: Patti's maroon Reliant went first to Cael, then to Nancy, next to Addie, and Clover finally drove it into the ground. Nancy's boyfriend Mike towed it away.

Food, however, is obviously unrecyclable. It comes in, it goes out. (And for those with septic systems, consider the wear on my septic field as our toilets get flushed dozens of times in a twenty-four-hour period.)

I'm not complaining, though. It's not only essential to eat well and have a full belly, it's important to have a full cupboard when kids open the door seeking sustenance in one form or another. More important than a new toy or a fancier car or a backyard pool or a trip to Club Med, a stocked refrigerator and cupboard help to make home feel nourishing, a place of respite from the widespread spiritual famine of contemporary life. Home is a sanctuary from the elements; it is where you break bread with those who share your hungry struggle; it is there where you quench your driving thirst and then tell of your day.

In nineties hip-hop psychology, it is generally understood that food is not love. But it is. It is a part of loving your children, feeding them until they are healthy enough and wise enough to learn how to feed themselves. Whatever the cost.

STOPPING BY THE WOODS

The enriching qualities of human frailty and sorrow

> *Therefore, it seems to me that everything that exists is good—death as well as life, sin as well as holiness, wisdom as well as folly.*
>
> —HERMANN HESSE

More than 150 years ago, the literary behemoths Dana, Alcott, Cooper, Poe, Longfellow, and Hawthorne were turning the reading world on its ear with their passionate writings about the human condition. Now they are all but extinct and forgotten. Their books are too slow, too long-winded, too full of pointless description for the contemporary mind.

Here it is almost 2000 A.D. and we do everything on the go and in pairs: eating takeout, driving while yapping on the cellular, laptopping on the train, reading on the toilet, even grabbing a few winks on the plane en route to meetings in cities we've never visited but go to all the time. We don't have time to read Poe's poignant "Tamerlane."

Contemporary life bears an odd resemblance to a day at Walt Disney World, where for the price of admission, you board the college-marriage-career-parenthood-camcorder-restaurant-movie-midlife-crisis ride and get dropped off at Condo-Land where Olive Oyl turns on the VCR and shows you scenes from a life you forgot you had lived. We do aerobics to relaxation tapes, jog to work, race to yoga classes, dash to shrinks, speed through quality sequences with kids and dogs and aging parents, and wake from sleepless nights to labor for bosses who want us to be in three places at one time. It's enough to make our collective heads spin.

Which brings me to Hawthorne's *The Scarlet Letter* and the perennial question from my students spread far too thin for their young years as to why I make them read it: simply stated, it cannot be read on the run or even at a slow trot.

No, one must sit down in order to have any hope of comprehending its multilayered story. It's a ponderous, repetitive, elusive, excruciatingly detailed drama where, I would be remiss not to admit, little happens. Two hundred fifty pages concerning the question of sin and what happens to our frail and sometimes sorrowful lives. It is humbling both for the oblique nature of its message and the inescapable truth of that message. It commands us to a halt.

Five years ago I watched fourteen-year-old Clover as she returned from soccer practice after school. On the way into the house that afternoon, the phone was ringing; she grabbed the receiver from Addie, and after some coded teenage preliminaries while scanning the refrigerator and paging through the catalogs left on the counter, Clover made hasty plans to meet some friends later that evening.

She was already leaping for the stairs when Elizabeth, our two-year-old with leather and metal braces on her tiny legs, let her big sister know she had a different notion. She just sat in the hall in front of Clover and held up her pink arms. And waited.

The message was inescapable. Clover ceased the forward momentum that had carried her almost nonstop from her first step onto a yellow school bus in 1981, the same force that would have propelled her and her contagious zest for life up the stairs and out of Elizabeth's grasp for at least another day.

But she actually stopped.

She picked up her baby sister, brought that wonderfully soft face to her cheek, kissed her, uttered a few silly words, retrieved the doll she wanted, and moments later, put her down. Not much happened, but Clover's life was once again changed forever by a complex little girl who directs the traffic of our speeding lives like a beefy cop.

At two years old, Elizabeth was still six months away from taking her first wobbly step, yet she commanded enormous power by asking or whining or crying or demanding or cajoling or literally shinnying up our legs. And she maintained an undaunted faith that one of us would always stop.

Every time she held up her hands we stopped.

We stopped to hold her. We stopped to change her. We stopped to carry her on our hip while we did a million and one other things that need doing. We stopped to pick her up, to simply touch her miraculously soft skin, to smell her sweet breath, to do what was important, to remember, to maintain our collective sanity.

Carrying a two-year-old with a metal brace on her legs strains your back beyond belief. Short on mobility and long on language development, she repeated herself endlessly. After spending a full day with her, we all discovered that nothing had happened and our brains were minus several million cells. Yet she became the powerful core of our lives.

Elizabeth Bayou-Grace was—and remains—a constant reminder that, despite all the endless scurrying around this globe with visions of our own puffed-up importance, the world does not work the way we expect it to, that there is sometimes unavoidable sorrow in our fragile lives—and that there is always a rare and wonderful kind of joy in acknowledging our helplessness in the face of all that.

That is why I make my students read Hawthorne.

IN DEFENSE OF LARGE FAMILIES

How more is less

All know that the drop merges into the ocean, but few know that the ocean merges into the drop.

—KABĪR

Soon after Clover was born, we began to notice the occasional raised eyebrow among friends. After all, we had three children already. Why more?

Danny arrived two years later with the first of the "jokes" about our sex life. With Bay's birth came the disapproving *tsks*, which, loosely translated, meant "Get a life." Mostly, I laughed. One of the great lessons of big family living is to not take things personally.

However, since Elizabeth graced our lives seven years ago, the occasional criticisms about "living large" have grown harsher and less easy to laugh off. The accusing fingers are pointed in various verbal and nonverbal ways, but they invariably say the same thing: *By your selfishness you're contributing to the world's hunger and pain.*

What do you say to that—especially when it's not said?

And so I've occasionally found myself driving aimlessly for hours around this small college town muttering to myself, answering my accusers, accusing my accusers, trying to find the perfect Rosanne-esque response to the barbs of people from global ecology groups who claim that big families—especially big American families—disproportionately use the world's rapidly diminishing natural resources.

The real problem for me has been that, on the surface, their accusations seem true: the overpopulated earth is growing smaller and more ravaged every day. One look at global population growth rates and it's hard to argue the point. And it is an undeniable fact that Americans simply take more, use more, need more, discard more, pollute more, and ultimately produce more ecological devastation than people anywhere else on earth. It all seems pretty simple.

But it's not. Another singularly important axiom learned from big family life is that nothing is ever simple. This was illustrated to me once again the other day in a seemingly insignificant moment when I saw twenty-year-old Addie scold little Elizabeth for leaving the refrigerator open—just as I or her mother would have done—and then watched as she put her younger sister's hair in braids and the two of them went out to the swings. No big deal, but the world suddenly grew larger. It was an amazing metaphysical event whereby an adolescent was transformed into an adult and, a few moments later, a little child.

And this evening, when I solemnly considered my brood scattered throughout this big house and across this vast country, I understood in that soulful place beyond understanding that there is a dimension of life that exists beyond the realm of numbers, of dollars and cents, of bottom lines and even predictable physical phenomena.

Under our roof there is, in abundance beyond reason, the essence of spirit on this planet. There is the spirit of so-loud-you-can't-think dinners, of tuna casserole realities, of sibling wars fought under tables and behind closed doors, of stealthily borrowed clothes, of never quite getting your fair share, your next turn, your rightful due. And then in the midst of all the furor that drives people and countries to war, there are countless acts of kindness and love that nourish, sustain, redeem, and ultimately expand the universe in which we live.

Going against all laws of physics, my kids, like many other children in solid large families, are simply capable of giving more than they take from the earth. My children understand in their bones what it's like to live under the same roof with many others. They understand better than most adults the economics of sharing. They know from countless meals about not taking more than you can eat. After a lifetime of tagging behind, they know how to follow; and after years of taking little ones by the hand, they know very well how to lead.

Although I can't substantiate it, I am certain that the future scientist—or psychologist or social engineer or basement inventor—who ultimately solves the problem of world overpopulation will come from a big family. (Probably the unbelievably squeezed middle child.) Few others on this planet understand the issues of crowding so intimately and so compassionately.

Only someone who is one of many would know the mystical mathematics involved in proving that more is less is more—that the ocean indeed merges into the drop.

BITING OFF THE MATTER WITH A SMILE

The remains of a Father's Day

> *Three Silences there are: the first of speech,*
> *The second of desire, the third of thought.*
> —HENRY WADSWORTH LONGFELLOW

A long time has rattled past since I saw the movie *The Remains of the Day*, but the face of Mr. Stevens, the butler played by Anthony Hopkins, has become one whose shaded eyes and strangled lips I recognize everywhere I go. I have seen him on Metro North trains, in coffee shops, leaning out of car windows. He once served me dinner in a dream.

To stir your memory, the slow-moving, understated film concerns an English butler whose devotion to a life of service keeps him alone, empty, and unfulfilled. He is a man whose dignity in this most undignified age would now be considered less a tragic flaw than an unremarkable character flaw. At the end of his day, all that remains is hollow intention.

It should have been utterly forgettable, yet I cannot escape the remains of that movie.

It was about my father, who devoted the soul of a lifetime to his business. It was about my good friend Steve, a building contractor, who carried on at work through the terrible darkness of his father's death; my nephew Jake in California, who wrote a painful story about a boy's inability to tell a girl he loved her; my closest pal in the world, a photographer who would never ask his famous movie star friend for a lead. It was about my dear sons, who, as they grow older, grow less able to cry out at the awful pain in life. Indeed, they grow less able to double over with laughter at the absurdity of it all.

It was about the silence of men; it was about the way fathers and their sons never really say what they mean.

And so, of course, it was about me, though to look at my raucous, unprivate life with seven children, a sensuous wife, and a healthy disrespect for rules, you'd think that I saw a different film from everyone else. I didn't.

The anecdote I am about to share is as silly and adolescent as it is middle-aged and stodgy, or even elderly and a bit confused. It is embarrassing to tell because it points out how petty I am, how imprisoned I am by my silence.

Some time ago a publisher of some renown bought a weekend place on our rural dead-end road. It was just cause for a lot of local gossip, not only because we suddenly had a celebrity neighbor but because everyone figured that our property values would increase. And I was privately thrilled because I'm a freelance writer. The serendipity of having a famous publisher as a neighbor seemed like suddenly going from fly fishing in a raging creek to dropping a line in a stocked pond.

Logic and reason—and my good wife—urged me to be simply neighborly: walk over there and introduce myself. Once on his doorstep, the fantasy goes, we would find a companionship of spirit. He would be mesmerized by my work and pass it on to his editors with *instructions*. Fame and fortune would be a commission away.

Yet several months passed and I did not walk the half mile to his house through the woods—I did not even know what the guy looked like. Whenever I replayed the neighborly visit scene in my head, it felt fawning. I was certain that he'd think me a phony for being friendly as a means of making a career move. (Of course, I would have been doing just that.) And I hated the thought of my kids seeing me pandering.

So I did nothing. And a few seasons later when I finally met the man by accident—I backed my Jeep (loaded with garbage) into his rental car!—I could not even use the coincidence to my advantage. We laughed about finally meeting "by accident," and he accepted my profuse apologies and we went our separate ways. He didn't say what he did for a living, and neither did I.

In retrospect, I guess it would have been okay to tell him simply that I am a writer, just as I suppose it would have been all right if someone spoke for the butler in the movie and told the maid that he loved her. I suppose. But not really.

After the movie last winter we met some friends at a local café. Each of the women said that they were frustrated and angry with the butler's unwillingness to give in to his emotions, to make that one step, to utter that one sound that would have gotten the Emma Thompson character to complete his life. Finally. But later my friend the building contractor leaned over and said that he wished the film had gone on for hours.

Me, too. A light had been turned on in my own private corridor of silence, and in the shadows I saw the faces of all the men I know. And I wanted to linger there in that quiet hall for a little while longer.

Every day since memory took root—back in the thickening darkness of my own private adolescence—I have had a sense of having to coerce myself through some flimsy curtain that separates me from all that I yearn for: companionship, love, acceptance, approval, joy.

Even now, nearly four decades later, I must urge myself—yes, bully myself on the darker days—through the thin gauzy folds as I come home each night from work to a house and a family I love with all my heart. And I do it. I do it. I do it because I must. I must. But at the risk of seeming overly dramatic (and, of course, a little less a man), it is always done with a sense of peril to my very identity, my sense of duty and dignity, my stubbornly protected privacy.

It is as if in coming home I find myself, like so many other fathers, stepping onto a stage of my fondest dreams, where the lights are suddenly too bright and the floor too slippery and the laughter too loud and the life too livid.

And I do it, although it would feel safer to disappear behind the newspaper. Or hide in the bathroom. Or find some dutied solace in work. The remains of a father's day.

WHEN BAD THINGS HAPPEN TO INNOCENT CHILDREN

What children really understand

> *I postpone death by living, by suffering, by error, by risking, by giving, by losing.*
>
> —ANAÏS NIN

At dinner some time ago, between forkfuls of pasta, Elizabeth asked me why anyone would blow up a day-care center full of children. She was talking about the infamous Oklahoma City bombing that took place in April 1995.

I was momentarily stunned, scurrying around behind a crooked smile trying to locate some wise and comforting fatherly words to counter the abject evil that had trespassed into her consciousness. Something that would blur the horrifying images of a bleeding child (or an abandoned doll or mangled scooter) that would linger long past the time that the TV screen went blank.

Although it was Oklahoma City that was on her young mind that night, I knew with terrifying clarity the moment I heard her question that there is a new nightmare every day to ponder for seven-year-olds who are full of questions about life—and death. If I could, I would have instantly erased the entire horrific episode from her memory the way you record over an old video, replacing the Stephen King movie with a cartoon. I'm her father. Her daddy. Her protector. That's my job, beyond all others. If I could I would shield her from all the terrifying images of contemporary life. I'd toss out the TV, radio, newspapers, magazines. No O. J. Simpson murder trial, no teenage blood on city streets, no victims of flesh-eating strep virus, no firemen carrying broken babies out of bombed-out buildings.

However, as the shocking scenes on the TV news every night remind each of us, large and small, there is no escaping the injustices in life, the dark truths that exist just beyond the smiley faces and rainbows painted on elementary school windows.

And that's what Elizabeth wanted to know: the truth. "Why, Daddy?"

"I don't know, Elizabeth," I said sadly, taking her hand, the soft, delicate fingers folded like a rose in my rough palm, hoping that was enough.

It was not. "But, have the bad men been caught? Can it happen again?"

I opened my mouth to soothe away her fears with a wishful lie ("I will never let anything hurt you, baby"). But Patti saved me from myself, telling her simply, gently, that there are good and evil people in the world, and adults try very hard to punish the evil ones and reward those who are good.

I watched Elizabeth's beautiful face closely, afraid that Patti had told her more than she could handle—or maybe not enough. But our amazing little girl just nodded and speared some more pasta. And that was that. She chattered on about Pogs and pee-wee baseball and her best friend, Kathleen, and along the way allowed me a glimpse into the simple truth that childhood innocence is, in large part, an adult invention. Of course. Who knows better than children just how small and powerless one can feel in this often cold and terrifying world?

When Elizabeth was just an infant she traveled through Keats's "vale of Soul-making." She knew even then. Now, like millions of other children, she goes to a school alongside kids with bald heads from cancer, kids who have been orphaned, kids who are abused. And when she returns each afternoon to her safe and warm home, she finds herself in the middle of the woods with copperheads in the grass, snapping turtles in the ponds, the terrifying screech of natural selection punctuating each and every day. She knows.

After dinner I held my little girl so close I wondered if she could hear the beating of my resilient and frightened heart. And then we went out into the yard for a few moments before dark because I think we both understood how important it is to laugh and play while we can. How terribly important to be part of a loving family that, although they can't protect you from pain, will stay with you until the ache finally goes away.

LOOKING OUT FOR NUMBER ONE, TWO, THREE . . .

Coming home

The one is none other than the All, the All none other than the one.

—SENG TS'AN

A lot of people tilt their heads and ask in that slightly uncomfortable—slightly accusatory—voice, "How can you keep track of so many kids?"

They smile teasingly and want to know if I always remember their names, their birth dates, their favorite foods, their homework assignments. (Yes.) Some wonder with a wry smile if we've ever forgotten one of them à la *Home Alone*. (Well, sometimes.) Others even have the temerity to ask in a whisper if each of our children was planned. (No.)

What they really want to know, however, is whether it's possible to love and care for seven children—or, more to the point, whether there's enough love to go around. *"Doesn't it all get used up by the time you have two or three (or at most four) kids?"* It's not a question, it's a challenge.

I usually smile and make a joke. I tell how I sometimes call one of the kids four or five names before I get to the right one— "Hey, Cael—Nancy—Addie—Clover—what's your name?—

Danny, please pass the bread." Or (for the umpteenth time this year) I recount the night we left Clover at the Vermilyes' house and didn't realize it until I counted heads in the van about five or ten miles down the road. Or the afternoon when Patti forgot that Cael was waiting for a ride at school and she, Clover, and Nancy went to the mall.

That's what most people want to hear. They certainly don't want a lengthy philosophical monologue about the logistics of managing children after they outnumber parents three or more to one. They want affirmation that they did the right thing by stopping at one or two or three.

They also want to confirm their suspicions about large families. As charming as the Waltons might have been—or the Bradfords from *Eight Is Enough*, or the Bradys—everyone knows that things are out of control in big families: we're sex-crazed, we're hiding from life behind our children, we're irresponsible, we're arrogant users of the world's resources, and, finally, the only thing that really matters, we can't possibly provide the love necessary for that many kids.

Yet the truth is that loving your big family is the easy part of having seven kids. In fact, there's nothing even remotely magical or metaphysical about it. It's not like there's a finite amount of parental love doled out to each individual at birth that later gets parceled out among the children—or that you somehow have to create precious love out of base metals so that there's enough to go around. Not at all. You simply love every one of your children with all your heart. That's it. Each one gets the same amount of love: your whole heart. (Which is not to say that you like all of them all the time—or even some of the time—you just love them without question.)

Two years ago Cael came home to the Hudson Valley from North Carolina for a quick visit. The same boy who couldn't wait to escape the pesty little urchins and his oppressive parents in 1987 to go a thousand miles away to college in Florida bought a cheap flight just to come here for a few days—to see eight-year-old Bay's Little League baseball game; to watch six-year-old Elizabeth's tap recital; to "chaperon" Danny's fifteenth birthday party; to pass big brotherly judgment on seventeen-year-old Clover's boyfriend, Jeffrey; to play a round of golf with the old man; to hang out at the local clubs with Nancy and Addie, who had just returned from college; to eat his mother's cooking; to lie back on the couch and watch the Knicks (while Bay and Elizabeth challenged his patience by continually walking in front of the tube).

To be where everyone loves him no matter what.

After the weekend I admit I was beat. As Cael's visit reminded me, with each additional child the house fills up not just by one but exponentially. It seemed that kids were everywhere; on all three floors of this big house—my kids, someone else's kids, kids I didn't even recognize. There were kids on the porches, kids in the refrigerator, kids in the bathrooms, kids on the phone, kids in my wallet, kids in the woods, kids in our bed; teenage boys sneaking a smoke outside the basement door, six-year-old girls leaving the hose running all night, seventeen-year-old girls returning empty juice cartons to the refrigerator, grown boys consuming the air, the couch, the TV, the CD player, the cold beer, even the floor space in the living room.

There was no escaping all of us. Which is just the point here. A big family is profoundly different from a small or even a "regular" family (which we experienced for a brief time between 1969 and 1974). In this house it's never ever about you alone; it's about everyone. Child rearing is not a piece of a grander life scheme; it's not a passage or a phase; it's not even the best part of life. In our time on earth there will be no neat divisions for Patti and me like the infant and toddler years, then the teenage years, then the empty nest years, then the grandparenting years. For us it is everything all at once. There is nothing else out there for us but this big family.

In fact it is so all-consuming—so inescapable—for me that I have come to understand that all my dreams of fame (vast riches, glorious adventure, etc.) are nothing more than fleeting distractions from the daily task of fathering this extraordinary brood. In the diminishing light of my fiftieth year, I see clearly that everything comes and everything goes except this inescapable family.

In an imploding universe where one must increasingly learn to go it alone, where survival depends upon one's ability to look out solely for number one, our children look out for each other. They come home because in a big family someone is always waiting for you.